CONVERSATIONS BETWEEN MEN

A Comprehensive Guide to
Decipher The Male Code,
Think like a Man, and
Build a Lasting Relationship with Him

NICCI BROCHARD
&
DR. BEN CHUBA

CONVERSATIONS BETWEEN MEN

A Comprehensive Guide to
Decipher the Male Code,
Think like a Man, and
Build A Lasting Relationship with Him

CROSSBORDER

New York, London, Quebec

CONTENT

Forward

Unlocking the Male Code

Relationships are the lifeblood of human connection, yet understanding each other often feels like trying to decode an ancient script. Women and men communicate in fundamentally different ways not better or worse, just different. Yet, these differences have led to centuries of frustration, miscommunication, and misunderstanding.

Men, by nature, often operate with an unspoken "code" a way of expressing emotions, handling stress, and navigating relationships that can sometimes seem puzzling, even elusive. Unlike women, who tend to articulate their feelings more openly, men often communicate through actions rather than words. What he says may not always reflect what he truly feels, and what he doesn't say may carry more meaning than what he does. This dynamic can leave many women feeling confused, unheard, or frustrated in their relationships.

This book is designed to be your guide to deciphering the male code; an inside look into how men think, why they act the way they do, and what they truly need in a relationship. It is not about changing yourself to accommodate a man, nor is it about manipulation. Instead, it is about understanding and bridging the communication gap so that you can build a relationship rooted in trust, connection, and mutual fulfillment.

Throughout these pages, we will break down the psychology of male communication, explore the ways men express love and commitment, and discuss how to cultivate a relationship that thrives on understanding rather than frustration. By learning to speak his language, you can foster a bond that is both deep and lasting; one where both partners feel seen, heard, and valued.

Are you ready to step into his world and truly connect? Join us (Nicci and Ben) to take this fascinating journey.

CHAPTER 1

Understanding the Male Communication Style

The Differences Between Male and Female Communication

Communication styles between men and women have long been studied, debated, and sometimes misunderstood. While individuals vary widely, general patterns emerge based on psychological, social, and even biological factors. Broadly speaking, women tend to engage in more expressive, detailed, and emotionally nuanced communication. They often use conversation to build rapport, express feelings, and explore complex social dynamics.

Men, on the other hand, often communicate in a way that prioritizes efficiency, problem-solving, and status management. This is not to say that men are incapable of emotional depth or that women cannot be concise; rather, these tendencies are shaped by a mixture of social expectations, evolution, and cognitive wiring.

Research suggests that women's brains have stronger connectivity between the left and right hemispheres, which facilitates multitasking and emotional expression in speech. Conversely, men's brains often show stronger connections within each hemisphere, leading to more compartmental thinking. This neurological difference may partially explain why men favor direct, task oriented communication and why emotional expression may sometimes be less verbal, and more action based.

Why Men Often Communicate Indirectly or Concisely

One of the most puzzling aspects of male communication is its tendency toward brevity. Many women wonder why men seem to respond with short, direct answers rather than elaborate discussions. The answer lies in both evolutionary and social roots.

Historically, men's roles in early human societies were often focused on tasks requiring strategic thinking and rapid decision-making such as hunting or defending territory. These activities necessitated communication that was brief, purposeful, and devoid of unnecessary elaboration. An excess of words could mean confusion or wasted time when swift action was needed.

In modern times, this evolutionary trait is reinforced by social conditioning. From a young age, boys are often encouraged to be assertive yet restrained in expressing emotions. Phrases like "boys don't cry" or "man up" subtly discourage emotional vulnerability, leading to communication styles that prioritize facts over feelings.

Another factor is how men often approach conversations as a means to an end, rather than as a process. They may engage in communication to exchange information, solve a problem, or establish authority rather than to explore emotions or deepen interpersonal connections. This can sometimes make their dialogue seem less engaging or responsive in casual conversation, but it does not mean they are uninterested. They are simply wired to focus on the essentials.

The Role of Social Conditioning in Shaping Male Dialogue

Social conditioning plays a significant role in defining how men communicate. From early childhood, societal expectations influence the way boys express themselves. In many cultures, verbal restraint is seen as a sign of strength, while excessive talkativeness, especially about emotions, is often discouraged.

Consider the difference in how boys and girls are often praised. Girls are frequently encouraged to express their thoughts, discuss their feelings, and engage in nurturing conversations. Boys, on the other hand, may receive praise for action based achievements rather than verbal expression. This early distinction subtly guides them toward a communication style that values action over words.

As men grow older, these learned behaviors manifest in professional and social settings. In workplaces, for example, men may favor direct and goal oriented communication, whereas women may approach discussions with a more relational and inclusive style. This does not mean one approach is superior; rather, understanding these differences can help bridge gaps in understanding.

Cultural influences also play a role. In some societies, masculinity is tightly associated with stoicism, further reinforcing the notion that men should communicate with restraint. In contrast, cultures that place a higher value on emotional expression may encourage a more open communication style among men.

How to Listen Beyond the Words for Deeper Meaning

One of the most valuable skills in understanding male communication is learning to listen beyond what is being said. Because men often communicate indirectly especially when it comes to emotions it is crucial to pay attention to tone, body language, and context.

For example, a man might not explicitly say, "I'm feeling overwhelmed," but he may exhibit signs of stress, such as withdrawing from conversations, becoming unusually quiet, or focusing intensely on a particular task. This indirect form of expression is not an attempt to be evasive but rather a deeply ingrained method of coping and communicating.

Men are also more likely to express emotions through actions rather than words. A father who fixes his daughter's car instead of saying, "I love you," or a husband who silently holds his wife's hand when she's upset may be demonstrating care in a way that feels more natural to him than verbal affirmation.

To truly understand male communication, it's important to observe patterns in behavior. What does he do when he's happy, stressed, or upset? Recognizing these nonverbal cues can provide a deeper insight into his thoughts and emotions, even when words are sparse.

Additionally, creating an environment where men feel safe to express themselves is key. Many men hesitate to share feelings because they fear judgment or appearing weak. Encouraging open dialogue without forcing expression can help build trust and lead to more meaningful conversations.

Recognizing When Silence is Communication

Silence is one of the most misunderstood aspects of male communication. While silence in a conversation may be uncomfortable for some, for many men, it serves a distinct purpose.

Men often use silence as a tool for processing thoughts. Unlike women, who may think out loud as a way of working through emotions, men tend to internalize their thoughts before speaking. This can sometimes create a perception that they are disinterested or disengaged, when in reality, they are carefully considering their words.

In conflict situations, silence can also be a means of de-escalation. Rather than engaging in emotionally charged discussions, many men retreat into silence to avoid saying something they may regret. This does not necessarily mean they do not care, but rather that they need time to process their emotions in solitude.

Furthermore, silence can be a form of support. Many men believe that simply being present is enough to convey understanding. For example, if a friend is going through a tough time, a man might choose to sit beside him without offering verbal comfort, believing that his presence alone communicates solidarity.

Understanding and respecting this aspect of male communication can prevent misinterpretations. Instead of assuming that silence indicates disinterest, it can be helpful to give space while gently inviting dialogue when the time feels right.

In Summary

Understanding male communication is not about labeling one style as better than another it is about recognizing differences and adapting accordingly. While men may communicate in ways that seem indirect, concise, or silent, there is often more happening beneath the surface.

By listening beyond words, acknowledging the role of social conditioning, and recognizing nonverbal cues, we can foster more meaningful interactions. Whether in relationships, friendships, or professional settings, appreciating the unique ways men express themselves can lead to deeper understanding and stronger connections.

The key takeaway? Communication is more than just words it's about intention, action, and interpretation. When we learn to see communication through multiple lenses, we gain the ability to truly connect.

CHAPTER 2

The Unspoken Male Code

The Importance of Loyalty and Respect in Male Interactions

Loyalty and respect are the foundation upon which male friendships and interactions are built. These two elements form the unspoken agreements that dictate how men interact with one another in various social settings. Unlike in other relationships where emotions and explicit affirmations are common, men often rely on actions to demonstrate their allegiance to one another.

Loyalty among men is often expressed through steadfastness, reliability, and discretion. It is the unbreakable understanding that, in times of need, one man can count on another without having to explicitly ask. This expectation exists in friendships, work environments, and even in casual social groups. Whether it is standing by a friend in a dispute or offering silent but solid support during difficult times, loyalty plays a crucial role in how men build and maintain their relationships.

Respect, on the other hand, is equally significant. It is often earned rather than given freely. Men value those who display competence, integrity, and strength whether that strength is physical, intellectual, or emotional. Disrespect, even in small doses, can be a significant breach of this unspoken code. Simple actions, such as interrupting, undermining a friend, or failing to acknowledge another's contributions, can lead to rifts that are difficult to mend.

How Men Express Emotions Without Words

Men have long been socialized to communicate their emotions in ways that differ from verbal expression. While many may assume that men are less emotional than women, the reality is that men simply display their emotions differently. Nonverbal communication plays a critical role in how men express feelings of affection, support, and even sorrow.

One of the primary ways men show emotion is through shared activities. Whether it is playing sports, working on a project, or simply sitting together in silence, these actions signify camaraderie and understanding. A father and son fixing a car together may not exchange many words, but the act itself is an unspoken bond of connection and care.

Physical gestures also convey deep emotions. A firm handshake, a clap on the back, or even a simple nod can hold a wealth of meaning. These actions replace the need for elaborate verbal expressions of appreciation, sympathy, or encouragement. When a man is struggling, a friend may not verbalize support, but a reassuring presence or a gesture of solidarity can be just as powerful.

In more serious moments, humor is often used as a tool to navigate emotions. A well-timed joke in a tense situation can serve to diffuse anxiety and provide comfort without requiring explicit emotional vulnerability. Similarly, shared laughter over past hardships can serve as an emotional release, creating an environment where men feel understood and supported without the need for direct emotional conversations.

Why Vulnerability Can Be Challenging for Men

Despite the strong connections that exist between male friends, vulnerability often remains a significant challenge. This difficulty stems from deeply ingrained societal expectations, personal upbringing, and the potential consequences of exposing one's emotions openly.

From an early age, many boys are taught that strength and resilience are paramount. Displays of vulnerability such as crying, expressing doubt, or seeking emotional reassurance are often met with discouragement. Phrases like "man up" or "don't be weak" reinforce the idea that emotional openness is synonymous with fragility, which many men strive to avoid.

Another contributing factor is the fear of judgment. Men worry that being vulnerable might be perceived as a sign of incompetence or inadequacy. In professional and social settings, they may fear losing the respect of their peers if they reveal personal struggles. This fear leads many to bottle up their emotions, choosing instead to deal with challenges internally or in ways that do not directly expose their deeper feelings.

Moreover, there is a lack of safe spaces where men feel comfortable being vulnerable. While women often have close circles where they can openly discuss their emotions, men are less likely to have such opportunities. Traditional male friendships revolve around shared activities rather than heart-to-heart conversations, making it difficult to introduce vulnerability into these relationships without feeling out of place.

The Hierarchy of Male Friendships and Social Structures

Male social groups often operate within a structured hierarchy that is based on a combination of respect, contribution, and influence. Unlike explicit rankings, these hierarchies develop naturally over time through unspoken rules and group dynamics.

At the top of many male social structures is the leader figure the person who exerts the most influence within the group. This individual is often the most confident, knowledgeable, or socially dominant. He may not necessarily be the loudest, but his opinions carry weight, and others look to him for guidance. The leader does not always assert his dominance outright; rather, it is subtly recognized by the group through their deference to his ideas and decisions.

Beneath the leader, there are core members those who have built strong relationships within the group and contribute significantly to its dynamics. These individuals are dependable and respected, playing crucial roles in maintaining group cohesion. They are often seen as trusted confidants and may act as mediators in disputes.

On the outer edges of the group are the peripheral members those who are part of the social circle but do not hold as much influence. They may be newer additions or individuals who do not participate as actively in group activities. While they are accepted, they may not be as deeply integrated into the group's social fabric.

This hierarchy is not rigid but is maintained through social interactions and unspoken understandings. It affects everything from decision-making within the group to the way members support one another. Understanding one's place in the hierarchy allows men to navigate friendships and social settings more effectively, ensuring smoother interactions and stronger bonds.

Unwritten Rules of Male Bonding

Male bonding follows a set of unwritten rules that govern how friendships are formed and maintained. These rules are not explicitly taught but are instead learned through experience and observation. They create an environment where men can connect without the pressure of verbalizing emotions or explaining their actions.

One key rule is the idea of "show, don't tell." In male friendships, actions often hold more significance than words. Loyalty, trust, and support are demonstrated through shared experiences rather than verbal affirmations. For example, a friend who shows up unasked when another is going through a tough time is demonstrating commitment without needing to say anything directly.

Another fundamental rule is the concept of "mutual respect through challenge." Men often bond by pushing each other whether through physical competition, friendly teasing, or intellectual debates. While this can sometimes appear confrontational, it is often a sign of camaraderie. These challenges serve as a way for men to test and strengthen their friendships while reinforcing mutual respect.

Additionally, the principle of "no excessive neediness" plays a role in how male friendships operate. While men rely on their friends for support, excessive emotional dependence is often discouraged. The expectation is that individuals should be capable of handling their problems independently while still knowing they can count on their friends if absolutely necessary.

Lastly, male bonding often relies on consistency over time rather than frequent emotional check-ins. Unlike female friendships, which may involve regular conversations about feelings and experiences, male friendships are often built on a long history of shared activities. A man may not speak to a friend for months, but when they reconnect, the bond remains unchanged.

Conclusion

The unspoken male code governs how men interact, communicate, and form bonds. Loyalty and respect serve as the pillars of male relationships, while nonverbal expressions of emotion allow for deep but often silent connections. Vulnerability remains a challenge, shaped by societal norms and personal fears, but it does not diminish the strength of male friendships. Social hierarchies play a subtle yet influential role in how men navigate their interactions, and unwritten rules guide the formation and maintenance of these bonds. While the methods may differ from those of other social structures, the depth and significance of male friendships remain just as profound.

CHAPTER 3
How Men Express Love and Affection

A Silent Declaration of Love

Mark sat at the kitchen table; his hands busy repairing the broken clasp of his wife's favorite necklace. He wasn't one for grand declarations or poetic words, but when Lisa came home from work that evening, she found the necklace sitting neatly on the counter, fixed and polished. She picked it up, running her fingers over the repaired clasp, and felt her heart swell. He hadn't said anything no "I love you" or "I missed you today." But in that moment, she understood. His love spoke through his hands, through his actions, and through the unspoken understanding between them.

This is how many men express love not through flowery language, but through quiet, deliberate action.

Why Men May Struggle with Verbal Expressions of Love

Societal norms, upbringing, and biological tendencies all contribute to why many men find it challenging to verbalize their emotions. From a young age, boys are often conditioned to prioritize strength, logic, and problem-solving over emotional openness. Phrases like "boys don't cry" or "man up" subtly discourage emotional vulnerability, leading to an adulthood where expressing feelings verbally feels foreign or even uncomfortable.

Additionally, psychological research has shown that male and female brains process emotions differently. While women tend to activate multiple areas of the brain associated with emotions and language, men often process emotions in a more compartmentalized manner. This means that while a woman might naturally articulate her feelings in words, a man might experience them just as deeply but struggle to find the language to express them.

However, this struggle does not mean that men feel less or love any less intensely. Instead, they often convey their emotions in different, less verbal ways that require understanding and interpretation.

Understanding Action Based Affection

For many men, love is something shown rather than spoken. This can be observed in their everyday actions taking care of things their loved ones need, fixing what's broken, offering help without being asked, or simply being present during tough times.

A man might express affection by:

- Ensuring his partner's car has gas before a long trip.
- Cooking a meal even if he's not a great cook, simply to take a burden off his partner.
- Doing small favors, like remembering her coffee order or making sure she has an extra blanket when it's cold.
- Supporting her quietly, standing by her side when she needs strength, even if he doesn't say much.

These acts, while seemingly simple, carry profound emotional weight. They are his way of saying, "I love you, I care for you, and I want to make your life better."

The Significance of Shared Experiences Over Words

Men often bond and express love through shared experiences rather than through words. A father who takes his child fishing, a husband who insists on watching his wife's favorite show with her, a friend who offers to help move furniture all of these are gestures of love and connection.

For men, quality time doesn't always require deep conversation. It can be about:

- Engaging in activities together, like hiking, playing a sport, or watching a movie.

- Building something side by side, whether it's a home project or a long-term goal.

- Simply being in the same room, sharing a comfortable silence.

A man may not always say, "I enjoy spending time with you," but his consistent presence speaks volumes. His willingness to participate in activities his partner enjoys whether or not they are his personal interests is an unspoken declaration of love.

Physical Touch and Its Role in Male Communication

While men may not always be verbal, physical touch is a powerful means of expression for many. Whether it's a reassuring hand on the back, an arm draped over a loved one's shoulder, or a lingering hug, touch often conveys what words fail to.

Physical gestures of love might include:

- Holding hands in public as a subconscious way of saying, "I'm here with you."

- Playful gestures like gentle teasing or affectionate nudges, which show comfort and connection.

- Protective actions, such as guiding a partner through a crowd or ensuring they walk on the safe side of the sidewalk.

- A simple but meaningful pat on the back or squeeze of the hand to show support and understanding.

For many men, these touches are deeply significant. They may not say "I love you" every day, but the warmth in their embrace, the security in their touch, and the way they instinctively reach out all communicate love in their own way.

When a Man Says Little but Means a Lot

There are moments when a man may say very little, but the depth of his feelings is undeniable.

For instance:

- A husband who quietly holds his wife's hand at a funeral, offering comfort without words.

- A father who wakes up early to warm up the car for his daughter on a cold morning before school.

- A partner who listens intently, nodding and responding with short but meaningful phrases, showing he values what's being said.

These moments of silence are often misunderstood as emotional detachment. However, for many men, these quiet gestures are their way of being present, offering support, and demonstrating love without the pressure of verbalization.

Bridging the Communication Gap

Understanding that men express love differently can help bridge gaps in relationships. Rather than expecting verbal affirmations, partners can learn to recognize the myriad ways in which love is displayed through actions, shared time, and physical touch.

At the same time, men can benefit from practicing verbal affirmation, even in small ways. Simple statements like "I appreciate you," "I'm glad you're here," or "You mean a lot to me" can go a long way in reinforcing emotional connection.

Likewise, partners of men who express love through actions can learn to acknowledge and appreciate these gestures, understanding that love does not always come in the form of words but can be deeply embedded in what one does.

Conclusion: Love Beyond Words

Society often equates love with verbal expression; it is important to remember that love is multifaceted. While some may communicate it through words, others demonstrate it through action, presence, and touch. Recognizing these different expressions of love allows for deeper understanding, stronger relationships, and a greater appreciation of the silent but powerful ways in which men convey their affection.

CHAPTER 4

Conflict and Resolution in Male Communication

Conflict is an inevitable part of human interactions, and the way individuals approach disagreements varies significantly based on numerous factors, including gender, social conditioning, and personal experiences. Male communication, in particular, often exhibits unique characteristics when it comes to handling disputes, with many men adopting distinct styles influenced by cultural expectations, emotional regulation, and personal values. This chapter explores how men approach disagreements differently, the reasons behind conflict avoidance or direct confrontation, the impact of ego and pride in male arguments, productive strategies for handling disputes, and the complexities of reconciliation and forgiveness in male relationships.

How Men Approach Disagreements Differently

The ways in which men handle disagreements can often be traced back to early socialization. From a young age, many boys are encouraged to display confidence, self-reliance, and assertiveness. As a result, their conflict resolution methods tend to reflect these learned behaviors. While some men prefer to assert dominance in disagreements, others may choose a more passive approach, depending on their personality and social environment.

Direct Confrontation vs. Indirect Resolution

One of the most significant differences in male approaches to disagreement is the distinction between direct confrontation and indirect resolution. Some men engage in direct verbal exchanges, clearly stating their opinions and standing firm in their arguments. This approach is common in competitive environments, such as workplaces, sports teams, and high stakes negotiations, where men feel the need to establish authority and maintain respect.

On the other hand, some men handle conflict through indirect resolution, avoiding outright confrontation while working to resolve disputes through actions rather than words. This might include making adjustments without discussion, relying on humor to diffuse tension, or waiting for emotions to subside before addressing the issue subtly. Understanding these differences is key to navigating male communication effectively, as forcing a direct confrontation on someone who prefers indirect methods may escalate the conflict rather than resolve it.

Why Some Men Avoid Conflict While Others Confront It Directly

The choice to avoid or confront conflict is shaped by a combination of personality, upbringing, and situational context. Several factors influence why some men choose to engage in disputes head-on, while others steer clear of confrontation whenever possible.

Social Conditioning and Cultural Expectations

Men raised in environments where aggression and assertiveness are praised may be more inclined to confront disagreements directly. In contrast, those who grew up in households or communities where harmony and composure were prioritized might develop a tendency to avoid conflict altogether. Cultural expectations also play a crucial role; in some societies, masculinity is associated with dominance and control, whereas in others, it is linked to patience and emotional restraint.

Emotional Regulation and Personal Experience

Men with strong emotional regulation skills may feel comfortable addressing disagreements directly because they trust their ability to remain calm and rational. Conversely, those who struggle with emotional control might avoid conflict due to the fear of losing their temper or saying something they later regret. Additionally, past experiences with conflict whether positive or negative can shape a man's approach. Someone who has seen conflicts escalate into damaging consequences may prefer avoidance, while those who have experienced constructive resolutions may be more willing to engage.

Power Dynamics and Perceived Risks

The dynamics of a relationship or situation often determine whether a man chooses to confront or avoid conflict. In professional settings, an employee may hesitate to challenge a superior, whereas among peers or subordinates, he might feel more comfortable expressing disagreement. Similarly, in romantic or familial relationships, men might avoid confrontation to maintain peace, especially if they perceive the issue as trivial or not worth the emotional toll.

The Role of Ego and Pride in Male Arguments

Ego and pride play crucial roles in male communication, particularly when conflicts arise. A man's sense of self-worth and identity can become deeply intertwined with his stance in an argument, making it difficult for him to back down or admit fault.

The Need to Be Right

For many men, being right in an argument is not just about the specific disagreement at hand but also about maintaining a sense of competence and authority. Acknowledging a mistake or conceding a point can feel like a blow to their confidence, leading some to double down on their positions even when presented with clear counterarguments.

Fear of Appearing Weak

Pride often prevents men from admitting when they are hurt, vulnerable, or wrong. In many social and professional circles, there is a stigma attached to appearing weak or uncertain. As a result, some men may adopt a defensive posture in disagreements, masking insecurities with aggression or dismissiveness.

Overcoming Ego in Conflict Resolution

To effectively manage conflicts involving male ego and pride, it is essential to create an environment where admitting fault is not equated with weakness. Encouraging open communication, emphasizing mutual respect, and focusing on problem-solving rather than personal attacks can help ease tensions. Additionally, allowing men to "save face" by framing concessions as collaborative solutions rather than personal defeats can make resolution more attainable.

Productive Ways to Handle Conflicts with a Man

Understanding the nuances of male communication allows for more effective conflict resolution. Employing strategic approaches can help navigate disagreements in a way that leads to constructive outcomes.

Choose the Right Time and Setting

Timing and environment play a significant role in resolving conflicts with men. Addressing issues when emotions are high can lead to defensive reactions, whereas choosing a calm, neutral setting increases the likelihood of a productive discussion. Private conversations are often preferable, as public confrontations can trigger a man's instinct to defend his reputation rather than engage in resolution.

Be Direct Yet Respectful

Men generally respond well to clear, direct communication. Rather than hinting at an issue or using passive-aggressive tactics, stating concerns in a straightforward yet respectful manner can lead to quicker resolutions. Using "I" statements (e.g., "I feel hurt when...") rather than accusatory language helps prevent defensiveness.

Focus on Solutions, Not Blame

Shifting the focus from assigning blame to finding solutions is particularly effective in male conflict resolution. Men often appreciate a pragmatic approach that centers on fixing the issue rather than dwelling on emotional grievances. Proposing actionable steps toward resolution keeps the conversation productive.

Allow Space for Processing

Some men need time to process disagreements before engaging in resolution. Pressuring immediate responses can lead to resistance or withdrawal. Giving space while signaling openness to discussion when they are ready can facilitate more meaningful dialogue.

Navigating Reconciliation and Forgiveness in Male Relationships

Once a conflict is addressed, the process of reconciliation and forgiveness follows. However, the way men approach this stage is often different from the way women do.

Nonverbal Reconciliation

Men frequently express reconciliation through actions rather than words. Instead of verbal apologies or prolonged discussions, they may demonstrate forgiveness through gestures such as resuming normal interactions, extending invitations, or engaging in shared activities. Recognizing these cues can help decipher when a man has moved past a conflict.

The Role of Time

Unlike more immediate emotional processing, some men prefer to let time heal wounds rather than dwell on apologies or discussions. While this can be frustrating for those who seek closure through dialogue, patience and understanding can go a long way in maintaining the relationship.

Encouraging Open Forgiveness

Though nonverbal reconciliation is common, encouraging verbal acknowledgment of forgiveness can strengthen relationships. Creating a safe space where apologies are given and received without shame allows for deeper connections and long-term harmony.

Avoiding Resentment

Unresolved resentment can quietly erode male relationships over time. Ensuring that conflicts are genuinely addressed rather than simply ignored prevents lingering bitterness. Encouraging honest discussions, even if brief, ensures that both parties feel heard and understood.

By recognizing the unique ways in which men handle disagreements and navigate reconciliation, conflicts can be managed more effectively, fostering stronger and healthier relationships.

CHAPTER 5

Emotional Intelligence and Men

Why Some Men Struggle with Emotional Vocabulary

Emotional intelligence, the ability to recognize, understand, and manage emotions effectively, is a skill that varies among individuals. Many men struggle with emotional vocabulary due to a combination of societal norms, upbringing, and personal experiences.

From a young age, boys are often socialized to believe that expressing emotions, particularly those associated with vulnerability such as sadness, fear, or affection, is a sign of weakness. Phrases like "man up" or "boys don't cry" discourage emotional openness, leading to a limited emotional vocabulary. Without the necessary language to articulate feelings, many men default to expressions of frustration or anger, which are more socially acceptable within the traditional construct of masculinity.

Additionally, family dynamics play a crucial role. If a boy grows up in an environment where emotional discussions are rare or discouraged, he may develop into a man who struggles to name and process his emotions. Without modeling from caregivers or role models who openly express their feelings, men often lack the tools to describe their inner emotional states.

Cultural influences further reinforce emotional suppression. Media, including movies and television, frequently depict men as stoic, problem solvers who prioritize logic over emotions. These portrayals contribute to an internalized belief that emotions should be secondary to reason, making it difficult for men to engage in emotionally expressive conversations.

Helping Men Open Up Without Pressure

Encouraging men to express their emotions requires patience and understanding. Many men are willing to discuss their feelings but need an environment that fosters openness without judgment or pressure. One effective approach is creating a safe space where emotional conversations feel natural rather than forced.

Active listening is a crucial component of this process. When engaging in conversations about emotions, it is important to validate a man's feelings without immediately offering solutions. Many men hesitate to share their vulnerabilities because they fear being seen as weak or incapable. By practicing empathy and allowing them to speak without interruptions or unsolicited advice, a sense of trust is built.

Timing and setting also influence a man's willingness to open up. Some men find it easier to discuss emotions during activities rather than in direct, face-to-face conversations. Engaging in shared activities such as walking, driving, or playing sports can create a relaxed atmosphere where discussions flow more naturally. Since eye contact can sometimes feel intimidating, side by side conversations allow for greater comfort.

Encouraging small steps rather than expecting deep emotional revelations all at once is also beneficial. Simple check-ins, such as "How was your day?" or "What's been on your mind lately?" can gradually lead to more meaningful discussions. By normalizing emotional dialogue over time, men feel more at ease sharing their thoughts and feelings.

Recognizing Emotional Suppression and Its Impact

Emotional suppression occurs when individuals consciously or unconsciously push down emotions rather than expressing them. In men, this suppression is often a learned behavior that stems from societal expectations, family conditioning, or personal experiences with rejection or invalidation.

One of the most common consequences of emotional suppression is stress accumulation. Suppressed emotions do not disappear; instead, they manifest in other ways, such as physical symptoms (headaches, muscle tension, fatigue) or psychological distress (anxiety, irritability, depression). Over time, these unresolved emotions can contribute to chronic health conditions, including high blood pressure and heart disease.

Furthermore, emotional suppression negatively affects relationships. When men struggle to express their emotions, their partners, friends, or family members may misinterpret their silence as indifference. This lack of communication can lead to misunderstandings, frustration, and emotional distance. The inability to share emotions can also make it difficult to resolve conflicts effectively, as suppressed emotions often resurface in unintended ways, such as passive aggressiveness or sudden outbursts of anger.

Workplace dynamics are also influenced by emotional suppression. Men who do not openly express their emotions may struggle with collaboration, conflict resolution, and leadership. In professional settings, the inability to communicate feelings effectively can lead to disengagement, burnout, or strained interactions with colleagues.

Recognizing emotional suppression requires self-awareness and external support. Men who have been conditioned to suppress their emotions may not immediately realize how it impacts their wellbeing. Encouraging mindfulness practices, journaling, or therapy can help men develop an awareness of their emotions and begin the process of healthy emotional expression.

Encouraging Healthy Emotional Expression

To counteract the effects of emotional suppression, men must learn and practice healthy emotional expression. This involves developing an understanding of their emotions, finding suitable outlets for expression, and surrounding themselves with supportive individuals who encourage openness.

One effective strategy is teaching men to identify emotions with specificity. Instead of using broad terms such as "stressed" or "upset," they can be encouraged to break down their feelings into more precise descriptions. Are they feeling overwhelmed, disappointed, frustrated, or misunderstood? Expanding their emotional vocabulary enables them to communicate their needs more effectively.

Engaging in expressive activities can also be beneficial. Some men may feel more comfortable expressing emotions through creative outlets such as music, writing, or art. Physical activities like sports, exercise, or martial arts can serve as constructive ways to process emotions, particularly for those who struggle with verbal communication.

Another essential component is fostering relationships where emotional expression is encouraged. Whether with a partner, a close friend, or a support group, having trusted individuals who actively listen and provide validation helps men feel comfortable sharing their emotions. Encouraging men to seek therapy or counseling can also be a transformative step, providing them with professional guidance on emotional intelligence and self-awareness.

Developing emotional expression is not just about talking; it is also about learning how to regulate emotions effectively. Men who struggle with expressing emotions often fear losing control. Teaching self-soothing techniques, such as deep breathing exercises, meditation, or cognitive reframing, empowers men to process their emotions in healthy ways rather than suppressing them.

How to Build Emotional Intimacy with a Man

Emotional intimacy is the foundation of deep and meaningful relationships. While many men desire emotional closeness, they may not always know how to cultivate it. Building emotional intimacy requires patience, trust, and consistent efforts from both partners.

One of the first steps in fostering emotional intimacy is demonstrating reliability and consistency. Men who have experienced emotional invalidation in the past may be hesitant to open up. Showing up consistently, keeping promises, and creating an atmosphere of trust helps them feel safe in sharing their emotions.

Another essential aspect is vulnerability. Emotional intimacy is a two-way street; it is difficult for a man to open up if his partner is not also willing to be vulnerable. By sharing personal thoughts, fears, and emotions, partners set a precedent for openness and honesty. This creates a mutual space where both individuals feel valued and understood.

Understanding and respecting communication styles is also key. Some men may not be as verbal in expressing emotions but may show love and connection through actions rather than words. Recognizing these different forms of emotional expression can prevent misunderstandings and ensure that both partners feel connected in ways that are meaningful to them.

Encouraging deep conversations without judgment is essential. Asking open-ended questions such as "What makes you feel appreciated?" or "What are your biggest fears?" can prompt deeper emotional exchanges. Creating rituals, such as weekly check-ins or dedicated quality time, can strengthen emotional bonds over time.

Lastly, practicing gratitude and affirmation reinforces emotional intimacy. Men, like anyone else, appreciate being acknowledged for their efforts and emotional openness. Complimenting their emotional growth, validating their feelings, and expressing appreciation fosters a supportive and loving environment where emotional intelligence can thrive.

Conclusion

Emotional intelligence is a skill that can be nurtured and developed in men, regardless of societal conditioning or past experiences. By understanding why some men struggle with emotional vocabulary, providing them with a safe space to open up, recognizing emotional suppression, and encouraging healthy emotional expression, we can help men build deeper emotional connections in their personal and professional lives. Ultimately, emotional intimacy is not about changing who someone is but about fostering a culture where emotions are acknowledged, understood, and valued as an integral part of the human experience.

CHAPTER 6

The Language of Masculine Vulnerability

Breaking the Stereotype That Men Don't Have Deep Emotions

For generations, societal norms have dictated that masculinity is defined by strength, stoicism, and an emotional reserve that prioritizes logic over sentiment. This stereotype, deeply ingrained in cultures across the world, has made it difficult for men to express vulnerability. However, the reality is that men experience emotions just as deeply as women, but they often communicate them in ways that are less immediately recognizable.

The notion that men do not possess complex emotional landscapes is a myth perpetuated by outdated ideas of masculinity. Emotions such as grief, love, fear, and disappointment exist in all human beings, regardless of gender. The difference lies in the conditioning men receive from an early age one that often discourages emotional expression and equates vulnerability with weakness.

Men, too, struggle with fears of rejection, inadequacy, and loss, but many have been conditioned to suppress these emotions or express them through alternative outlets such as humor, aggression, or detachment. The challenge is not in the existence of deep emotions but in how they are manifested. Understanding the language of masculine vulnerability requires dismantling the stereotype that men are emotionally shallow and recognizing the ways in which they do, in fact, express their feelings.

Recognizing When a Man Is Opening Up in His Own Way

Since men are often not socialized to express emotions in overt or conventional ways, their vulnerability may emerge in subtler forms. While women may feel comfortable verbalizing their emotions directly, men may express vulnerability through actions rather than words. For instance, a man might share a personal anecdote about a past failure or struggle without explicitly labeling it as emotional distress. He might also engage in deep conversations about topics that resonate with his experiences rather than speaking directly about his own feelings.

Another key indicator of a man opening up is his willingness to let his guard down in ways that go beyond words. He may invite someone into his personal space, share meaningful music or literature, or display nonverbal cues such as prolonged eye contact, a change in tone, or a shift in body language. Recognizing these signals is crucial in understanding how men communicate their emotions.

Moreover, humor can often serve as a defense mechanism as well as a gateway to vulnerability. Some men will mask their true feelings with jokes or sarcasm, testing the waters before fully revealing what they feel. If they sense that their emotions are being met with understanding rather than judgment, they may feel more comfortable sharing their innermost thoughts.

How Men Test Trust Before Revealing Emotions

Trust plays a critical role in male vulnerability. Many men have been conditioned to view emotional openness as risky something that could be used against them or diminish their perceived strength. As a result, they often employ subtle tests to determine whether they are in a safe environment before exposing their emotions.

One common way men test trust is through small disclosures. They may begin by sharing minor frustrations or challenges to gauge the listener's response. If their concerns are met with ridicule, dismissal, or discomfort, they are unlikely to take the risk of revealing more significant emotions. Conversely, if their feelings are acknowledged and validated, they may gradually open up further.

Men may also assess trustworthiness through actions rather than words. They might observe whether someone keeps their confidences or how they react to the emotions of others. A person who is judgmental or dismissive of another's vulnerability is unlikely to be seen as a safe space for emotional expression.

Another way men test trust is by using humor or indirect communication. They might make self-deprecating remarks about their struggles to see whether the listener reacts with empathy or indifference. If they sense genuine concern and understanding, they may be more willing to share openly.

The Connection Between Self-worth and Vulnerability in Men

A man's ability to express vulnerability is often closely tied to his sense of self-worth. When a man feels secure in himself, he is more likely to embrace vulnerability as a strength rather than a weakness. However, if he struggles with self-doubt, he may fear that revealing his emotions will make him appear inadequate or unworthy.

For many men, self-worth is deeply intertwined with their perceived ability to provide, protect, and succeed. When they feel they are failing in these areas, their instinct may be to withdraw or mask their emotions rather than express them. This is why societal messages that equate masculinity with toughness can be particularly damaging when men internalize the belief that vulnerability makes them weak, they may suppress their emotions to maintain a sense of self-respect.

Encouraging men to embrace vulnerability requires reinforcing the idea that emotional openness is not a sign of weakness but of strength. When men are given the space to express their emotions without fear of judgment, they can begin to develop a healthier relationship with their own self-worth. This process is often gradual, requiring patience, support, and a willingness to challenge deeply ingrained beliefs about masculinity.

Creating a Safe Space for Honest Conversations

One of the most powerful ways to help men embrace vulnerability is by creating an environment where they feel safe expressing their emotions. This requires more than just telling them that it is okay to open up it involves demonstrating, through actions and responses, that their emotions will be met with understanding and support.

Active listening is key to fostering a safe space for men to be vulnerable. This means not interrupting, not offering unsolicited advice, and not rushing to fix their problems. Instead, listening with empathy, asking thoughtful questions, and acknowledging their feelings can help them feel seen and heard.

It is also important to avoid pressuring men into sharing before they are ready. Vulnerability is a deep personal journey and forcing it can have the opposite effect. Instead, creating opportunities for open dialogue whether through shared activities, casual conversations, or simply being present can encourage men to express themselves in their own time and way.

Additionally, normalizing emotional expression among men can help break the cycle of suppression. When men see other men being open about their feelings without negative consequences, it reinforces the idea that vulnerability is acceptable and even beneficial. This can be done through role models, media representation, and cultural shifts that challenge outdated notions of masculinity.

In conclusion, the language of masculine vulnerability is complex and often misunderstood. By breaking the stereotype that men do not have deep emotions, recognizing the ways in which they express vulnerability, understanding how they test trust, addressing the link between self-worth and emotional openness, and creating a safe space for honest conversations, we can encourage a healthier and more authentic form of emotional expression among men. In doing so, we pave the way for stronger relationships, deeper connections, and a society where vulnerability is recognized as a sign of true strength.

CHAPTER 7

Navigating Relationship Expectations with Men

Anecdote: The Tale of Emma and David

E mma had always believed in love that balanced independence with companionship. She met David, a passionate entrepreneur who thrived on his own terms. In the beginning, their relationship was effortless. They spent hours talking, laughing, and planning future adventures. However, as time passed, Emma noticed that David would withdraw for days at a time, immersed in his projects. She felt neglected, while he felt pressured. It wasn't until they sat down to discuss their expectations and fears that they began to truly understand one another. Through this, Emma learned that a man's need for independence does not necessarily mean he does not value the relationship. Similarly, David realized that closeness does not equate to losing oneself. Their story is a testament to the delicate balance required in navigating relationship expectations with men.

Understanding His Need for Independence vs. Closeness

Men often grapple with a fundamental internal conflict: the desire for intimacy and connection versus the need for personal space and autonomy. In relationships, some men may naturally gravitate toward moments of solitude to recharge, while others seek emotional closeness to feel secure. Understanding this dynamic is crucial in maintaining a healthy relationship.

One of the most common misinterpretations occurs when a partner mistakes a man's need for space as a withdrawal of love. In reality, many men process emotions differently than women, often retreating to sort out their thoughts before reengaging. Recognizing this as a pattern rather than a rejection can prevent misunderstandings and unnecessary conflicts.

To navigate this, communication is key. Instead of assuming that his retreat signifies disinterest, approach him with curiosity and patience. Discuss boundaries and personal time and find a middle ground that satisfies both partners' needs. Closeness should not suffocate, and independence should not breed distance. A healthy relationship flourishes when both partners respect and support each other's individual rhythms.

How Societal Roles Influence a Man's Relationship Expectations

Society plays a powerful role in shaping a man's expectations in relationships. From an early age, boys are often taught to be providers, protectors, and problem solvers. As they grow into men, these expectations can manifest in relationships in various ways sometimes as a sense of responsibility, sometimes as emotional guardedness.

In many cultures, men are expected to suppress vulnerability and maintain a stoic presence. This can create challenges in relationships, as emotional expression is often necessary for deep and meaningful connections. When a man struggles to articulate his feelings, it is not always due to a lack of emotion but rather a conditioned response to avoid appearing weak.

To bridge this gap, fostering an environment of openness and acceptance is essential. Encouraging emotional expression without judgment can help break down societal barriers. Rather than pressuring a man to communicate in ways that feel unnatural to him, providing reassurance that vulnerability is not only acceptable but welcomed can lead to more profound emotional intimacy. Recognizing these ingrained roles allows both partners to challenge outdated expectations and cultivate a relationship based on authenticity rather than social constructs.

Why Some Men Fear Commitment and How to Address It

The fear of commitment is a complex issue, often rooted in past experiences, societal pressures, or personal insecurities. Some men associate commitment with a loss of freedom, while others fear emotional vulnerability or potential failure.

One of the primary reasons men fear commitment is the pressure of long-term responsibility. Society has long depicted commitment as a life altering decision that requires complete sacrifice. This perception can make some men hesitant to settle down, fearing that they may lose aspects of their individuality or autonomy in the process.

Additionally, past relationships play a significant role. A man who has experienced betrayal, heartbreak, or toxic dynamics may carry emotional scars that make him hesitant to invest fully in a new relationship. The fear of repeating past mistakes or getting hurt can act as an invisible barrier, preventing deeper connections.

Addressing this fear requires patience and understanding. It is crucial to create a relationship built on trust, allowing him to feel secure rather than trapped. Open conversations about expectations, concerns, and long term goals can help dispel uncertainties. Rather than demanding commitment, fostering an environment where commitment feels like a natural progression rather than an obligation can make all the difference.

The Importance of Mutual Respect in Decision-making

Respect is the cornerstone of any healthy relationship. When making decisions as a couple, mutual respect ensures that both partners feel heard, valued, and considered. Unfortunately, many relationships falter when one partner dominates decision-making while the other feels sidelined.

In relationships with men, traditional gender roles often position them as the primary decision-makers, especially in financial, career, or major life choices. However, a truly equitable partnership involves both voices carrying equal weight.

To foster mutual respect, it is important to establish an open dialogue where both partners contribute to decision-making processes. This does not mean that every choice must be a lengthy debate, but rather that each person's perspective is acknowledged and valued.

Encouraging a dynamic where decisions are made collaboratively strengthens trust and partnership. When both partners feel they have a say in their shared journey, resentment diminishes, and the relationship thrives. Respect is not about agreement in every situation; it is about acknowledging and considering each other's viewpoints as valid and significant.

Supporting His Ambitions Without Losing Your Own Identity

One of the most delicate aspects of a relationship is finding the balance between supporting a partner's dreams while ensuring personal aspirations are not sidelined. Many women find themselves in the role of a cheerleader encouraging their partner's goals, celebrating their victories, and providing emotional support. While this is a beautiful expression of love, it should not come at the cost of one's own identity.

A relationship should be a partnership of mutual encouragement. Supporting a man's ambitions does not mean sacrificing personal goals, nor should it mean diminishing one's own growth. Instead, both partners should empower each other to reach their full potential.

The key lies in setting boundaries and maintaining individual pursuits. Engage in discussions about career aspirations, personal growth, and shared dreams. Encourage one another but also ensure that personal achievements are recognized and valued equally.

In thriving relationships, both partners inspire and uplift each other. The healthiest love stories are those where both individuals can stand tall, knowing they have not lost themselves in the process of supporting another.

Conclusion

Navigating relationship expectations with men requires patience, understanding, and open communication. By recognizing the balance between independence and closeness, challenging societal norms, addressing fears of commitment, fostering mutual respect, and supporting each other's ambitions, relationships can grow stronger and more fulfilling. A successful relationship is not about changing a partner but about understanding and evolving together. When both individuals feel seen, heard, and valued, love can flourish in its most authentic form.

CHAPTER 8

When a Man Pulls Away: What It Means and What to Do

Decoding Withdrawal: Stress, Fear, or Uncertainty?

When a man begins to pull away, it can be an alarming and confusing experience. The initial instinct might be to blame yourself, assume the worst, or react emotionally. However, withdrawal does not always signify the end of a relationship. Understanding why men retreat is crucial in determining how to respond appropriately.

Men withdraw for various reasons, often tied to their internal world rather than the dynamics of the relationship. One of the most common reasons is stress. Unlike many women, who may seek support and conversation to cope with stress, men frequently process their struggles internally. They may distance themselves as a way to manage overwhelming emotions, work pressure, family concerns, or personal struggles.

Another major factor is fear. Fear of commitment, vulnerability, or failure in the relationship can cause a man to step back. If he is not emotionally prepared to handle deepening intimacy, he may instinctively create space to reassess his emotions. This does not necessarily mean he does not care but rather that he is grappling with uncertainty about the future of the relationship.

Uncertainty, in general, can be a significant reason why a man withdraws. He may be questioning his feelings, evaluating whether he sees a long-term future, or even dealing with unresolved past relationship traumas. In some cases, this period of withdrawal serves as a personal reflection, helping him gain clarity about his emotions and priorities.

The Difference Between Needing Space and Losing Interest

It is vital to differentiate between a man who is seeking space and one who is losing interest. The way he behaves during withdrawal often provides clues about his true intentions.

A man who needs space will still show signs of care and investment in the relationship. He may be less communicative but still responsive. His tone, when he does interact, will remain respectful and warm. He may assure you that he is dealing with personal matters and that his withdrawal is not about you but rather about his own struggles.

On the other hand, a man who is losing interest will display different behaviors. His communication will become infrequent and lack depth. His responses may feel indifferent or forced, and he may make excuses to avoid spending time together. The energy he once put into the relationship will diminish, and you may sense a growing emotional distance.

Understanding this distinction is crucial because it helps you determine the appropriate response. If he genuinely needs space, pressuring him may do more harm than good. If he is losing interest, however, it may be time to reassess the relationship's future.

How to Respond Without Pushing Him Further Away

Once you recognize that a man is withdrawing, how you respond can make a significant difference in whether he returns or continues to distance himself. Here are some key strategies to navigate this situation:

- **Give Him the Space He Needs** – If he is withdrawing because of stress, fear, or uncertainty, the best approach is to respect his need for space. Avoid bombarding him with messages or demanding immediate explanations. Instead, let him know you're there for him when he's ready to talk and allow him to process his emotions in his own time.

- **Maintain Your Emotional Balance** – It is easy to let fear and insecurity take over when someone pulls away. However, responding with neediness, panic, or ultimatums can push him further away. Instead, focus on maintaining your emotional balance. Engage in activities you enjoy, spend time with friends, and remind yourself of your own worth.

- **Communicate Calmly and Clearly** – If the withdrawal continues and begins to affect the relationship significantly, addressing it in a calm and non-accusatory way can help. Express your concerns without making him feel trapped. For example, you might say, "I've noticed you've been distant lately. I care about you and just want to make sure you're okay."

- **Avoid Overanalyzing and Making Assumptions** – When a man withdraws, it is easy to jump to conclusions about what it means. However, overanalyzing his every action or interpreting silence as rejection can create unnecessary anxiety. Instead, focus on what you do know and trust that clarity will come with time.

- **Focus on Your Own Well-being** – One of the most empowering things you can do in this situation is to prioritize yourself. Take this time to engage in self-care, invest in your personal growth, and ensure that your happiness is not solely dependent on his attention or affection.

When to Wait and When to Walk Away

Not all withdrawals lead to the end of a relationship, but some do signal a deeper issue that should not be ignored. Knowing when to wait and when to walk away is an essential skill in preserving your emotional wellbeing.

When to Wait:

- If he communicates that he needs time but still reassures you of his feelings.

- If his withdrawal is due to external stressors rather than a lack of interest.

- If he continues to show signs of care and effort, even if they are less frequent.

- If he eventually returns and is willing to discuss what caused his distance.

When to Walk Away:

- If he repeatedly withdraws without explanation or reassurance.

- If his actions consistently show disinterest or lack of respect.

- If you feel emotionally neglected and unappreciated in the relationship.

- If he refuses to communicate or acknowledge your concerns over an extended period.

Walking away is not about punishing him but about protecting yourself. If his behavior shows that he is not willing or capable of maintaining a healthy relationship, it may be in your best interest to let go and open yourself up to someone who values and reciprocates your love.

The Importance of Self-Respect in These Situations

One of the most significant aspects of handling a man's withdrawal is maintaining your self-respect. Your worth is not determined by whether or not he chooses to stay or go. Rather, it is reflected in how you handle yourself during these moments of uncertainty.

Self-respect means refusing to chase someone who is unwilling to communicate or invest in the relationship. It means recognizing your value and setting healthy boundaries. When you operate from a place of confidence and self-worth, you are less likely to tolerate behavior that leaves you feeling anxious, unwanted, or undervalued.

A relationship should be a partnership, not a one-sided effort where you constantly fight for someone's attention and affection. By holding yourself to high standards, you naturally attract a partner who values and appreciates you for who you are.

Conclusive Thoughts

When a man pulls away, it can feel unsettling, but it does not always signify the end of a relationship. Understanding the reasons behind his withdrawal, differentiating between needing space and losing interest, and responding with emotional intelligence can help you navigate this challenge effectively. However, your self-respect and emotional wellbeing should always remain the priority. If a relationship continually leaves you feeling uncertain, unappreciated, or emotionally drained, then the best decision may be to walk away and invest in a connection that aligns with your self-worth and happiness.

CHAPTER 9

Thinking Like a Man: Strengthening Your Connection

The Silent Drive

Lena and Marcus had been together for five years. One evening, after a long day at work, they were driving home in silence.

Lena felt something was off. She wanted to ask, "What's wrong?" but hesitated, knowing Marcus often needed space to process his thoughts. Instead, she took a deep breath and let the quiet settle between them.

Minutes passed, and then Marcus finally spoke. "I had a rough meeting today. I just need to think things through."

Lena nodded, understanding that her partner wasn't shutting her out he was sorting things out in his head. It was a small moment, but it reinforced an important lesson: men often process emotions differently. They need time, space, and logic to navigate their feelings. Learning to recognize and respect that was key to strengthening their bond.

Understanding His Priorities and How He Processes Emotions

Men and women often have different ways of processing emotions. While women may prefer talking things out as a way to work through their feelings, men tend to internalize, analyze, and compartmentalize before expressing themselves.

From an evolutionary standpoint, men have been conditioned to focus on problem-solving and efficiency. This doesn't mean they don't feel deeply it simply means their emotional processing operates differently. Instead of seeking immediate emotional validation, they might prefer to first assess whether an emotion requires action.

For example, if a man is upset about a work-related issue, he may not immediately discuss his feelings. Instead, he might distance himself from the situation until he has formulated a logical response. Recognizing this tendency allows for patience and support rather than misinterpreting his silence as disinterest.

One way to navigate this dynamic is to allow space while still signaling support. Rather than asking repeatedly if something is wrong, a simple "I'm here if you need to talk" can be more effective. This approach respects his processing style while still keeping the lines of communication open.

Why Logic Often Trumps Emotion in Male Decision-Making

Many men default to logic over emotion when making decisions, which can sometimes create misunderstandings in relationships. This inclination doesn't mean they lack empathy; rather, it reflects their desire for efficiency and structure.

In decision-making, men often prioritize the following:

- **Problem-Solving:** They prefer finding a solution rather than dwelling on emotional aspects.

- **Risk Assessment:** Their choices are often based on calculated risks and practical benefits.

- **Long Term Stability:** Decisions are influenced by the potential for long term success rather than temporary emotional satisfaction.

Understanding this can prevent frustration when discussing issues in a relationship. For example, if a woman is venting about a difficult situation, a man's first instinct might be to offer solutions rather than simply listening for emotional support. This response isn't meant to dismiss emotions but to address the perceived problem.

A useful strategy is to communicate expectations clearly. If emotional support is needed, saying, "I just need to vent, not fix this," helps set the right tone. By bridging this gap in communication styles, partners can avoid misunderstandings and work together more effectively.

How to Engage in Discussions That Resonate with Him

Effective communication with a man requires an approach that aligns with his natural thought process. Here are some key strategies:

1. **Be Direct and Concise:** Men tend to appreciate clarity. Long, emotionally detailed conversations can sometimes overwhelm them, making it harder for them to respond effectively.

   - Instead of saying, "I feel like we never spend time together anymore, and I don't know if you even want to anymore," try, "Can we set a date night every week? I miss our time together."

2. **Frame Conversations Around Solutions:** If you want to discuss a problem, presenting it with possible solutions helps maintain engagement.

   o Rather than saying, "You never help around the house," try, "Could we set a schedule for chores so we can balance things better?"

3. **Give Him Time to Process:** Not all discussions need immediate answers. Some men need to mull things over before responding meaningfully. Allowing space for that can lead to more productive conversations.

4. **Use Action-Oriented Language:** Men often respond better to statements that involve clear actions rather than abstract emotions.

   o Instead of, "I feel unappreciated," try, "I'd love it if you acknowledged the little things I do. It makes me feel valued."

By fine-tuning discussions to align with his communication preferences, interactions become more effective and fulfilling.

The Role of Shared Interests in Deepening Bonds

One of the most effective ways to strengthen a relationship is through shared interests. While emotional connection is vital, having common activities fosters companionship and partnership.

Men often form connections through action rather than conversation. Engaging in activities together whether it's hiking, watching sports, cooking, or playing video games builds a natural bond without the pressure of constant verbal communication.

How to Cultivate Shared Interests:

- **Explore His Hobbies:** Even if his interests aren't initially appealing, trying them out can lead to new experiences and a deeper connection.

- **Find New Activities Together:** Discovering mutual interests, like traveling or fitness, ensures ongoing engagement in the relationship.

- **Respect Individual Preferences:** While sharing activities is important, allowing space for independent interests strengthens mutual respect and personal fulfillment.

When a man feels that his partner enjoys spending time with him in ways that are meaningful to him, he naturally feels more connected.

Encouraging Open Communication Without Pressure

While fostering emotional openness is crucial, forcing deep conversations prematurely can backfire. Many men may be less inclined to verbalize emotions openly, especially if they feel pressured. Instead, creating an environment where they feel safe and respected encourages natural emotional sharing.

Tips for Encouraging Open Communication:

- **Choose the Right Moments:** Timing matters. Heavy conversations are best approached when both partners are relaxed and not overwhelmed with stress.

- **Use Non-Confrontational Language:** Phrasing matters. Instead of, "You never tell me how you feel," try, "I love hearing about your day what was the best part of it?"

- **Acknowledge His Efforts:** When he does open up, even in small ways, reinforcing that behavior with appreciation makes it easier for him to continue doing so.

- **Lead by Example:** Demonstrating vulnerability without expectation encourages reciprocation. If you share your thoughts openly but without demanding a response, it naturally creates space for him to do the same.

Encouraging communication without pressure ensures that he feels comfortable expressing himself in a way that aligns with his personality.

Conclusion: Bridging the Gap for a Stronger Connection

Understanding a man's perspective doesn't mean changing who you are it means recognizing differences in emotional processing, decision-making, and communication styles to foster a stronger connection.

By acknowledging his natural tendencies, engaging in shared activities, and creating a safe space for communication, a deeper and more fulfilling bond can be built. The key lies in balance respecting his ways of thinking while also ensuring your needs are met. When both partners work together in this way, relationships flourish, strengthening the emotional and intellectual connection that sustains long-term love.

CHAPTER 10
Building a Lasting Relationship with Him

Afulfilling and enduring relationship doesn't happen by chance; it is nurtured through intentional actions, deep understanding, and mutual respect. While love can be spontaneous, sustaining a meaningful connection requires effort, adaptability, and patience. This chapter explores the essential pillars of a lasting relationship finding the right balance between independence and togetherness, establishing trust and consistency, growing together through challenges, appreciating how he expresses love, and embracing the ever evolving journey of connection.

The Balance of Independence and Togetherness

A strong relationship thrives on both intimacy and individuality. Many couples struggle with finding the right equilibrium between being deeply connected and maintaining their personal identities. Too much togetherness can lead to a sense of suffocation, while too much independence can create emotional distance.

Healthy relationships encourage both partners to pursue their individual passions, friendships, and goals while still prioritizing time together. When both individuals maintain their personal growth, they bring more energy, excitement, and wisdom into the relationship. This fosters a sense of admiration for each other as independent beings, preventing dependency or resentment.

Striking this balance begins with open communication. Talk about your needs whether you require personal space to recharge, time for hobbies, or moments for self-reflection. Similarly, make it clear when you need quality time together. Scheduling date nights, sharing daily experiences, or engaging in common interests strengthens the bond while still allowing room for personal fulfillment.

Another aspect of maintaining independence within a relationship is supporting each other's ambitions. Encouraging his career, personal projects, or self-improvement efforts shows that you value him as an individual, not just as a partner. In turn, receiving the same support fosters a dynamic where both partners grow individually without feeling threatened by each other's successes.

How Trust and Consistency Create Emotional Security

At the heart of every lasting relationship is trust. It is the foundation upon which emotional security is built, allowing love to deepen without fear or hesitation. Trust is not simply given it is earned through consistency, reliability, and transparency.

Consistency reassures a partner that they are valued, loved, and considered in the other's actions. When words and actions align over time, it creates a stable environment where both partners feel emotionally safe. If, however, promises are frequently broken or behaviors are unpredictable, doubt and insecurity creep in, weakening the relationship.

Trust is also nurtured through honesty and openness. Being forthcoming about thoughts, emotions, and concerns prevents misunderstandings and eliminates unnecessary conflicts. A strong relationship does not require perfection but rather a willingness to be vulnerable and truthful. Whether it's discussing financial decisions, personal fears, or relationship expectations, transparency strengthens the bond.

Additionally, trust grows when both partners demonstrate that they can rely on each other. Showing up during difficult times, being a consistent source of support, and fulfilling commitments all contribute to emotional security. Knowing that your partner will stand by you through life's ups and downs provides a sense of peace that strengthens the relationship over time.

Growing Together Through Life's Challenges

Every couple will face challenges financial stress, family dynamics, career changes, health concerns, or emotional hardships. What sets strong relationships apart is how partners navigate these difficulties together. Instead of allowing obstacles to drive a wedge between them, they use adversity as a means to grow stronger.

One of the keys to overcoming challenges is teamwork. Approaching problems as a unit rather than as adversaries fosters a sense of "we" rather than "me vs. you." When both partners share a problem-solving mindset, they work collaboratively instead of blaming each other. Discussing issues with openness and finding mutually beneficial solutions strengthens the bond and promotes resilience.

Another essential element in growing together is practicing patience and understanding. Difficult times can bring out stress, frustration, or insecurities, but responding with empathy rather than judgment makes a significant difference. Offering emotional support and reassurance during hardships creates an environment where both partners feel safe expressing vulnerabilities.

Moreover, learning from challenges rather than avoiding them contributes to personal and relational growth. Viewing difficulties as opportunities for deeper understanding, improved communication, and strengthened commitment allows a couple to evolve positively. Growth requires discomfort at times, but the lessons learned during struggles often lead to a more profound and lasting connection.

Recognizing and Appreciating His Way of Showing Love

Love is expressed in countless ways, and every individual has their own unique way of showing affection. While some people are vocal about their love, others may demonstrate it through actions rather than words. Understanding and appreciating how your partner expresses love can prevent misinterpretations and unmet expectations.

One way to recognize his expressions of love is by identifying his love language. He may prioritize acts of service doing things for you, fixing things around the house, or ensuring your comfort. Others may show love through physical touch, quality time, verbal affirmations, or thoughtful gestures. Acknowledging these efforts, even if they are different from your own way of expressing love, enhances appreciation and emotional connection.

Sometimes, love is shown in quiet, subtle ways. It may be in how he remembers the little details about you, checks in on you during a busy day, or sacrifices something small to make you happy. Instead of expecting love to always be demonstrated in grand or overt ways, paying attention to these small but meaningful gestures can help you feel more valued and connected.

Equally important is expressing gratitude for these efforts. When you acknowledge and appreciate his ways of showing love, it encourages him to continue expressing affection in his natural way. If you feel that your needs for affection or validation are not being met, open and gentle communication can help bridge any gaps without making your partner feel inadequate.

Our Final Words on Embracing the Journey of Connection

A lasting relationship is not a destination but a continuous journey of discovery, adaptation, and deepening love. As time passes, both individuals will evolve, and so will the dynamics of the relationship. The key to longevity is embracing this evolution with an open heart and a willingness to grow together.

Challenges, changes, and uncertainties are inevitable, but what matters most is the commitment to navigate them together. Choosing love every day through small acts of kindness, open communication, mutual support, and shared dreams creates a foundation that withstands time.

Ultimately, a meaningful relationship is not about perfection but about the effort and intention behind every interaction. Cherish the moments of joy, learn from difficulties, and never stop investing in the connection. The beauty of love lies in its depth, and the more you nurture it, the stronger it becomes.

By embracing the complexities and beauty of a lasting relationship, you cultivate a bond that is not only enduring but deeply fulfilling.

CHAPTER 11

The Male Brain: A Map of Motives, Wiring, and Responses

I. The Biological Blueprint: Hormones, Brain Structure, and the Chemistry of Behavior

When we talk about the male brain, it's not about stereotyping or generalizing it's about understanding the biological canvas upon which every man's unique story is painted. While every individual is shaped by personality, upbringing, culture, and experience, there are core biological elements that influence how men think, feel, and act. This section unpacks those elements with curiosity and clarity.

At the heart of the male brain's wiring are a few key hormones testosterone, dopamine, and vasopressin being the big players. Testosterone, often misunderstood as simply the "aggression hormone," is actually more like a highlighter pen on male behavior. It sharpens traits like competitiveness, assertiveness, and even protective instincts. Testosterone levels fluctuate throughout a man's life and even within a single day, influencing energy levels, focus, mood, and even risk taking behavior.

Dopamine, the brain's reward chemical, is also particularly responsive in males. Research shows that male brains tend to have a stronger dopamine-driven "seeking system" which means they're often more motivated by the thrill of novelty, challenge, or accomplishment. This doesn't mean women don't seek rewards it just means men are, on average, more biologically wired to pursue them in different ways, often through action and conquest rather than social bonding.

And then there's the architecture of the male brain itself. MRI studies have shown structural differences between male and female brains particularly in the amygdala (responsible for emotion and fear response) and the prefrontal cortex (the planning, impulse control, and decision-making hub). While the male amygdala tends to be larger, the female brain shows greater interconnectivity between hemispheres. This contributes to observable differences in how each gender processes emotional information. Men may be less likely to verbalize emotion, not because they feel less, but because the pathways between emotional and language centers in the brain are less directly connected.

Also important: the male stress response. Men typically experience a "fight or flight" reaction, thanks to higher levels of vasopressin and a faster reacting amygdala. This affects how they react to confrontation, pressure, or emotional intensity not because they lack empathy, but because their brain instinctively prepares for action rather than introspection in stressful moments.

Understanding this biological framework doesn't box men in it frees us to meet them where they are. It opens the door to interpreting silence not as detachment, but as a different kind of emotional processing. It helps decode a partner's focus on tasks, achievements, or external goals not as avoidance, but as expressions of identity and contribution.

II. Evolution's Echo: Instincts of Protection, Provision, and Status

Beyond biology, there's evolution. While we no longer live in caves or fend off saber toothed tigers, our brains are still shaped by the survival roles our ancestors played. And for men, those roles largely centered around protection, provision, and competition for status.

At the core of male evolutionary wiring is the need to protect and provide. Thousands of years of evolutionary pressure ingrained in men a hyperawareness of threat and a drive to secure safety not just physical, but also emotional and social. This is why men often express love or loyalty through action. Think fixing something around the house, offering solutions when you vent, or taking the lead in risky situations. These behaviors are rooted in the protective instinct that helped their ancestors survive and pass on their genes.

Provision the desire to bring resources to the table is also deeply encoded. In modern times, that might translate into ambition, career drive, or the pursuit of financial security. Even men who reject traditional roles often feel an internal tug to *contribute* in a tangible, practical way. When men worry about losing their job or underperforming, the panic isn't just about money it can feel like a threat to their identity.

Then there's competition. In the ancestral world, a man's success at gaining status (through strength, skill, or intelligence) affected his ability to attract mates and protect his tribe. Fast forward to today, and that ancient instinct still plays out on the basketball court, in boardrooms, and even in casual debates with friends. The need to win, to be seen, to earn respect: it's not always about ego. It's about wiring.

Of course, evolution isn't an excuse for bad behavior. It's not a hall pass for aggression, control, or detachment. But it does help us understand the *why* behind some modern male tendencies especially those that can feel confusing or frustrating in intimate relationships. When a man shuts down instead of sharing, focuses on fixing rather than listening, or gets defensive when criticized, what we're often witnessing is a mix of ancient instincts and modern expectations colliding.

By recognizing these evolutionary influences, we learn how to navigate them more compassionately not by indulging outdated dynamics, but by addressing them with awareness, curiosity, and updated tools for communication.

III. Processing the World: Attention, Emotion, and Communication Styles

Have you ever wondered why some men seem laser focused on one thing while missing emotional cues all around them? Or why a heartfelt conversation might end with him suggesting a to-do list instead of offering comfort? These behaviors can often be traced back to differences in how the male brain processes information.

Let's start with attention. The male brain is generally more geared toward "systemizing" than "empathizing." That means men are often drawn to how things work, patterns, logic, and cause-effect relationships. They may prefer direct tasks over nuance and are typically more likely to zone in on a single issue rather than juggle emotional variables. This doesn't make men less capable of empathy it just means empathy may not be their default lens.

This single focus tendency is mirrored in what researchers call the "male brain's task orientation." While women often approach conversations to connect emotionally, men often approach them to solve problems. So when a woman says, "I'm overwhelmed," and a man responds with "Here's what you should do," he's not trying to dismiss her feelings. He's responding in the way his brain has been wired and often socialized to help through action.

Then there's emotion. Contrary to myth, men are not less emotional. But they do tend to process emotions more internally and may struggle with emotional labeling. The connection between the amygdala (emotion center) and the verbal centers in the male brain is less active than in women's brains, which helps explain why many men can feel deeply without having the same fluency in expressing those emotions.

This creates a common relational dynamic: one partner wanting emotional expression and verbal validation, and the other seeming aloof or unengaged not because he doesn't care, but because he doesn't know how to bridge the internal to the external. This can be especially challenging in conflict, where the male brain is more likely to enter a "shutdown" mode retreating not out of indifference but out of neurological overwhelm.

Communication styles reflect all of this. Men often prefer clear, direct exchanges, especially when under stress. They may see tangents or emotional exploration as confusing or inefficient. This can lead to misinterpretations: a woman might think he's being cold or dismissive, while he might feel like he's trying to be helpful and getting punished for it.

Understanding these patterns doesn't mean we abandon emotional depth. It means we learn to speak each other's language, appreciate different forms of connection, and work toward a shared emotional vocabulary that respects both partners' wiring.

IV. The Socialization Layer: Conditioning, Masculinity Norms, and Emotional Suppression

If biology and evolution are the blueprint, then socialization is the interior design. Every man is shaped not just by his genes and instincts, but also by the messages he receives from the world around him. And from a young age, those messages often teach boys that certain feelings are off limits.

"Big boys don't cry."

"Be a man."

"Don't be weak."

These phrases aren't harmless. They carve deep grooves in the male psyche, teaching boys to suppress vulnerability, deny emotional need, and equate strength with stoicism. By the time boys become men, many have internalized the idea that showing emotion especially sadness, fear, or tenderness is a risk to their masculinity.

This suppression doesn't erase emotion; it just pushes it underground. As a result, many men carry emotional burdens that go unnamed and unprocessed, sometimes erupting in ways they themselves don't understand. Anxiety becomes anger. Shame becomes withdrawal. Grief becomes distraction.

And it's not just about emotion it's about identity. The modern man is often caught in a tug-of-war between outdated masculine ideals and emerging expectations of emotional intelligence and vulnerability. He may want to be open, communicative, and empathetic but feel unequipped or afraid of being judged.

Workplace dynamics add another layer. In environments that reward dominance and competition, emotional openness can feel risky. Many men learn to compartmentalize to excel professionally while staying guarded emotionally. And in romantic relationships, this can lead to intimacy gaps that frustrate both partners.

The good news? Conditioning can be unlearned. When men are given safe spaces to explore their inner world, when they're met with curiosity instead of criticism, and when vulnerability is seen as strength, remarkable emotional growth can happen. But it requires a cultural shift one that starts with understanding, not blame.

V. Toward Deeper Connection: Translating Male Psychology into Practical Insight

Understanding the male brain isn't just about decoding men it's about building bridges. When we understand how men are wired, conditioned, and motivated, we can create more compassionate, effective ways to connect, communicate, and collaborate. Whether you're a partner, friend, parent, colleague, or just someone curious about human nature, this insight empowers you to engage with empathy and skill.

Here are some takeaways:

- **Emotionally, men may need more time and safety to open up.** That doesn't mean they're emotionally unavailable it means they're emotionally cautious. The more they trust that their vulnerability won't be judged, the more likely they are to share.

- **Action is often their language of love.** If a man fixes your car, brings you coffee, or helps you move he's speaking affection through behavior. Learn to recognize and appreciate these gestures, even if they're not verbal.

- **Silence isn't always withdrawal.** Men often process internally. Giving space, while signaling presence, can go further than pushing for immediate verbal response.

- **Criticism feels deeply personal even when it's not meant to be.** Because male self-worth is often tied to performance and provision, they may hear "you did this wrong" as "you're not enough." Framing feedback with reassurance ("I know you care, and here's something that would help me feel even more connected...") can make a huge difference.

- **Encouraging emotional literacy is a gift.** Whether it's naming feelings, modeling vulnerability, or simply asking thoughtful questions ("What was the hardest part of your day?"), you're helping rewire decades of conditioning.

Ultimately, this chapter isn't about excuses it's about expansion. It's about widening the lens on what it means to be male, moving beyond clichés and toward a more nuanced, respectful understanding. When we grasp the interplay between hormones, structure, instinct, and conditioning, we stop expecting men to behave like women or punishing them when they don't. Instead, we meet them in their reality, with tools that foster connection, not confusion.

CHAPTER 12

What Men Talk About When They Talk About Women

I. Beyond the Surface: The Real Terrain of Male Conversations

There's a cultural myth that when men talk about women, it's all jokes, objectification, or emotionally shallow commentary. We've been fed the stereotype of the locker room chat: crude, simplistic, and detached. But that narrative misses the mark. While some male conversations about women may skim the surface, many dig far deeper into realms of admiration, fear, confusion, respect, vulnerability, and emotional complexity.

What men say about women when women aren't in the room tells us as much about their emotional landscape as it does about their relationships. Across interviews and social listening sessions, a wide spectrum emerges. Yes, there are moments of humor and bravado, but they often coexist with raw admissions: "I don't know how to talk to her anymore," "She intimidates me in the best way," or "I still think about the one that got away."

These conversations often occur in safe male circles friendships forged over time, with enough trust for emotional honesty. The stereotype of male emotional suppression is not entirely inaccurate, but it's incomplete. The truth is, men *do* talk they just do it differently, often indirectly. A joke might carry a compliment. A silence might carry heartbreak. A "she's cool" might carry admiration so deep it's hard to articulate.

Take, for example, the way men discuss their partners when their guard is down. Many express awe: "I don't know how she does it all," or "She sees right through me." Others confess fear not of women themselves, but of not being enough, of not being able to provide emotionally or live up to expectations.

And let's not forget the younger generation. Gen Z men are growing up with greater emotional literacy, exposure to mental health dialogue, and shifting gender norms. Their conversations, while still sometimes laced with bravado, are increasingly emotionally rich. One 23 year old shared, "She made me realize I've been numbing myself to avoid getting hurt again." That's not locker room talk. That's a real life reflection.

So while the loudest male voices in pop culture might project bravado, underneath that is a quieter truth: many men are thinking, processing, and feeling a lot more than they let on. And when they talk about women, they're often revealing just as much about themselves.

II. Love, Lust, and Limbo: How Men Navigate Attraction and Emotion

One of the most common threads in male conversations about women is the navigation of attraction how it forms, what sustains it, and what complicates it. But unlike the trope that men are only driven by physical desire, many conversations reveal the inner tug-of-war between *chemistry* and *connection*, between *desire* and *depth*.

Let's start with the undeniable: men do talk about physical attraction. It's a real, visceral part of the male experience, and it often sparks initial interest. But very quickly, deeper questions arise especially in more emotionally aware male circles. Conversations move toward: "What's she like?" "Is she cool to talk to?" "Can I be myself around her?" These aren't just checklists they're emotional barometers.

Some men, especially in their 20s and 30s, talk about a kind of "attraction fatigue" where the thrill of newness wears off quickly if emotional connection isn't there. One man put it this way: "I used to chase what looked good. Now I'm chasing what feels like peace."

Others speak about the tension between *what they want* and *what they're afraid of.* A surprising number of men admit that being around confident, emotionally secure women both draws them in and makes them feel exposed. "She doesn't need me to rescue her," one man said with a mix of admiration and vulnerability. "That's a good thing. But it also makes me wonder what I bring to the table."

Conversations about sex also carry nuance. While some are lighthearted or playful, many reflect a desire for mutuality and meaning. Emotional safety matters, even if men don't always have the vocabulary to describe it. "When I trust her," one man said, "everything's different. I can show up as myself, not just some performance."

There's also an honest exploration of limbo the undefined space where attraction hasn't turned into clarity. Men talk about "situationships," ghosting, mixed signals, and the anxiety of not knowing where they stand. These conversations often reveal emotional vulnerability beneath a mask of casualness. "She says we're just hanging out," one guy shared, "but I think about her way more than I should. I just don't know how to ask for more without scaring her off."

These emotional limbos are fertile ground for growth but also for confusion. Men are often unsure how to bridge the gap between emotional longing and societal expectations around stoicism and detachment.

III. Heartbreak, Hesitation, and the Ghosts of Past Relationships

When men talk about women, heartbreak is a recurring theme. But unlike the open sob sessions often depicted in female friendships, male discussions of emotional pain are quieter, more veiled, and sometimes more enduring.

Many men carry unprocessed heartbreak for years. They don't always talk about it directly, but it shows up in casual mentions, shifts in tone, and reflective moments. "There was someone," a man might say. Or "She changed the way I see love." In these moments, their emotional world comes sharply into view.

What's striking is how long these emotional wounds can linger. While women often move through breakups with a support network, men frequently cope alone or with minimal emotional processing. Some turn inward. Others jump quickly into new relationships, still echoing the voice of the past. One man admitted, "Every time I get close to someone, I compare her to the one I lost."

Conversations also reveal a powerful tension between desire for connection and fear of vulnerability. Many men express hesitancy around commitment not because they're emotionally unavailable, but because they're emotionally *wounded*. They fear repeating past mistakes, disappointing someone they care about, or exposing themselves to pain again.

Some of this stems from early relationships that shaped their view of love. One man recounted, "My first girlfriend cheated on me. I've never fully trusted someone since." Others speak about relationships that ended without closure, leaving them stuck in a cycle of avoidance and self-doubt.

Interestingly, male conversations about exes often include respect and admiration. "She was incredible," they might say. "I messed it up." There's guilt. There's nostalgia. And there's often a deep awareness of personal growth: "I wasn't ready back then. I see it now."

What these conversations reveal is that heartbreak doesn't harden men as much as it quiets them. It makes them more cautious, less expressive. But the pain is still there waiting for a safe space to be shared, validated, and released.

This emotional residue can either block new love or become the groundwork for deeper relationships depending on how it's processed. When men talk about women from their past, they're not just reminiscing. They're mourning, learning, and sometimes hoping.

IV. Masculinity, Vulnerability, and the Search for Emotional Safety

In many male conversations about women, there's an underlying theme: the search for emotional safety. For men raised in cultures that equate masculinity with stoicism, the experience of feeling emotionally safe with a woman can be transformative and terrifying.

Men talk about the women who "get them" who don't just tolerate their vulnerability but *welcome* it. "She saw through my walls," one man said, "and didn't run away." That kind of acceptance is rare, and when it happens, it often becomes the benchmark for future relationships.

But the road to vulnerability is filled with detours. Many men fear that emotional openness will be used against them. They've heard stories or lived them of being vulnerable and then dismissed, mocked, or left. This fear doesn't come from fragility; it comes from experience.

That's why men often test emotional waters slowly. They drop hints. They joke about serious things. They offer partial truths and watch how they're received. If the response feels safe, they open up more. If it doesn't, they retreat.

This isn't manipulation it's self-preservation.

Men also talk about the paradox of being expected to be both strong and emotionally available. "I'm supposed to be the rock," one man said, "but also pour out my heart. Sometimes I don't know which one she wants."

There's also discussion around power dynamics. Some men feel emotionally outpaced by their partners, unsure how to keep up with emotional expression or depth. Others feel pressure to perform a pressure that shows up not just in bed, but in conversations, decision-making, and even daily life.

What they long for, many say, is *mutual vulnerability* a space where both people can show up fully, without fear of judgment or dismissal. They want to be partners, not just providers. They want to be known, not just admired.

And here's the kicker: many men are more ready for emotional intimacy than we think. They just don't always know how to ask for it. Their conversations are often coded, their admissions subtle. But the longing is real.

If women are taught to hide their strength, men are often taught to hide their *softness*. But that softness is where love, trust, and real connection are born. And when a woman helps a man reclaim it, it's not just relationship changing its life changing.

V. Generational Shifts and the Evolution of Male Dialogue

The way men talk about women is changing. Dramatically. And nowhere is that more evident than in generational differences.

Older generations Baby Boomers and Gen X often grew up in environments where emotional expression was discouraged, and gender roles were more rigid. Their conversations about women may have geared more toward status, physical appeal, or role expectations. Vulnerability existed, but it was usually private.

But younger men especially Millennials and Gen Z are rewriting the script. Raised in a world more open to mental health, gender fluidity, and emotional intelligence, their dialogues are far more nuanced. They're more likely to talk about feelings, therapy, communication breakdowns, and even gender dynamics with surprising depth.

One 21 year old shared: "We talk about love like we talk about music what it makes us feel, where it takes us." For them, masculinity is not defined by detachment but by *presence*. They want to understand, grow, and relate sometimes fumblingly, but authentically.

Social media has also influenced male dialogue. Platforms like Reddit, TikTok, and Instagram have become spaces where men share emotional insights, ask for advice, and open up about heartbreak. These platforms serve as informal group therapy where memes spark reflection, and comment sections become confessionals.

Of course, not all change is smooth. There's still backlash, confusion, and fear. Some men resist these shifts, holding tightly to traditional roles. Others feel caught between worlds wanting emotional fluency but unsure how to achieve it.

Mentorship matters here. Older men who've embraced vulnerability can guide younger men. Friend groups that prioritize honesty over performance create ripples of change. Romantic partners who model compassion over criticism help shape new emotional landscapes.

What's clear is this: we are living in a moment of transition. Male dialogue about women is evolving from objectification to admiration, from confusion to curiosity, from fear to trust. It's not perfect, and it's not complete. But it's happening. And it's beautiful to witness.

Conclusion: The Unspoken Depth of Male Dialogue

When men talk about women, they reveal much more than opinions about the opposite sex. They reveal who they are, what they value, what scares them, and what they hope for. These conversations are layered, coded, emotional, and real.

From the pain of heartbreak to the awe of being truly seen, from jokes that mask longing to hesitations born of past wounds, male dialogues about women are rich terrain. They are filled with insights, ironies, and the quiet hope that someone will understand them not just for what they say, but for what they mean.

And if we listen closely, without judgment or assumption, we might just hear the heartbeat of a new masculinity one that loves deeply, listens bravely, and speaks with a voice finally it.

CHAPTER 13

How to Make Male Friends Breaking the Code of Brotherhood

I. The Friendship Drought: Why Male Bonds Are So Rare Yet So Needed

In a world more connected than ever, an alarming number of men report feeling emotionally isolated. They have colleagues, workout partners, gaming buddies but very few people they can turn to in moments of vulnerability. The "friendship drought" among adult men is not just anecdotal; it's a documented social phenomenon with deep psychological roots and serious consequences.

So why is forming male friendships in adulthood so complex?

For many, it starts with early socialization. Boys are taught from a young age to prioritize strength over sensitivity, autonomy over intimacy. Emotional openness is often associated with weakness, and as a result, many boys are subtly steered away from the very skills that make friendship possible like expressing feelings, offering empathy, or asking for help.

As men age, these habits calcify. The competitive nature of school, sports, and eventually the workplace reinforces a relational model built on comparison rather than connection. By the time many men reach their 30s or 40s, they may find themselves surrounded by acquaintances but starved for real friendship. They can talk about fantasy football or career moves but not their fears, dreams, or grief.

Life logistics add another layer. Careers, marriages, fatherhood, and relocations shrink the pool of available time and emotional bandwidth. Unlike women, who are often socialized to maintain friendships as essential life infrastructure, men are subtly told that friendship is optional something nice to have, but not necessary. The result? Millions of men walking around with a quiet ache for connection and no roadmap for how to build it.

Yet, when male friendships do form and especially when they deepen they're powerful. Studies show that strong friendships reduce anxiety, boost emotional resilience, and even improve physical health. Men with close friends are more likely to cope well with stress, live longer, and experience a greater sense of purpose. Brotherhood is not a luxury; it's a lifeline.

This chapter is about reclaiming that lifeline. It's about naming the barriers, rewriting the scripts, and giving men and those who care about them the tools to build friendships that are not only real but transformative.

II. Shoulder to Shoulder: The Unique Style of Male Bonding

When it comes to friendship styles, there's a key distinction often drawn by psychologists: *face-to-face* vs. *shoulder to shoulder* connection. While many women bond through direct conversation sharing emotions, exchanging stories men often bond through shared activity. They do things together. Play sports. Work on projects. Go for drives. Tinker, compete, or build. The talking may come but it's often indirect, layered into the rhythm of doing.

This doesn't mean men are incapable of emotional connection. Quite the opposite. It means the gateway to that connection is often *action* rather than *introspection*.

Picture two friends fishing on a quiet lake. They might spend hours together with only sporadic conversation. But in those silences interrupted by laughter, teasing, or the shared satisfaction of the day trust builds. Emotional safety grows. Vulnerability tiptoes in.

This bonding style can be incredibly effective but also limiting. If emotional dialogue never emerges, friendships can remain stuck at the "buddy" level: fun, functional, but not deeply supportive. That's why learning to *read the signals* within shoulder to shoulder friendship is essential. These include small openings like:

- **Self-deprecating jokes** (hinting at insecurity)

- **Long pauses** (inviting space to go deeper)

- Mentions of stress, work, or family tension (emotional green lights)

- **Invitations to hang out again soon** (a sign of relational investment)

Men often express closeness not through direct affirmation but through loyalty, consistency, or protective gestures. "He was there when I needed him" becomes the highest praise. These coded behaviors are the foundation of what we might call the *language of male camaraderie.*

For men looking to build deeper friendships, the trick is to *translate* these actions into invitations for more depth. You don't need to demand a soul baring conversation. You just need to create enough relational gravity for it to happen naturally.

That might mean inviting a friend to join you on a long drive, a home improvement project, or even a regular pickup game and then using those settings to sprinkle in honesty. You start small: "Work's been kicking my ass." Or "Been thinking a lot lately." And see if it opens the door.

Men don't need to change their style to deepen their friendships. They just need to stretch it. Activity can still be the entry point but with just a bit more intentionality, it can lead to incredible emotional connection.

III. Cracking the Code: From Casual to Close

One of the most common frustrations men express is knowing *how* to take a friendship from casual to meaningful. They may have people they see regularly at the gym, in a fantasy league, or through work but conversations remain surface level. The transition to deeper friendship feels awkward, risky, or just plain confusing.

The first step is recognizing emotional green lights. These are moments when another man signals a willingness or even a desire for greater connection. It might look like:

- Sharing a personal story without prompting
- Asking a thoughtful question
- Reaching out unprompted
- Mentioning stress or change ("My dad's been sick lately...")
- Complimenting your character or actions ("You handled that well, man")

These are *not* throwaway moments. They're invitations.

The key is to *reciprocate without overwhelming*. Many men fear that going "too deep, too fast" will scare the other guy off. And they're not wrong there's a social tempo to male friendship that rewards steady pacing. That's why it's better to meet vulnerability with *matching vulnerability*. He opens up a little; you mirror it. He hints at a struggle; you share a relatable one. Over time, these micro moments build intimacy.

It also helps to name your intentions indirectly. Instead of saying, "I want to be close friends," which might sound awkward, try:

- "You're one of the few people I feel I can talk to."

- "I've been trying to get better about staying connected."

- "Good hangs like this don't come around often. Let's not let it slide."

These are ways of saying, I value this. I want more of this. You matter to me.

Another key practice: consistency. Male friendships often fade not from conflict but from neglect. Life gets busy, routines shift, and without intentional maintenance, even meaningful friendships drift. Creating rituals helps. A weekly game night, monthly catchup, or even just a regular text check-in can serve as anchors that hold the friendship in place.

Building closeness also means *showing up when it counts* birthdays, breakups, job losses, big wins. These are the emotional high tides when friendship either sinks or solidifies. Presence during these moments says, "I see you." And for many men, that's the most important sentence never spoken.

IV. Rewiring the Narrative: Friendship, Masculinity, and Emotional Courage

If male friendship seems elusive, it's not because men are emotionally stunted it's because culture has made emotional courage a taboo. From childhood onward, many men are subtly or overtly taught that closeness with other men is suspect, weak, or even unmanly. The very tools needed to build friendship are framed as threats to masculinity.

This is where we need to do cultural rewiring. Brotherhood is not about perfection or performative toughness it's about emotional presence, shared respect, and earned trust. And in today's world, it requires *courage* to pursue.

We live in a time where vulnerability is more accepted, but the scripts are still catching up. Many men feel the ache for connection but lack models of how to achieve it. Popular media either idolizes lone wolves or offers bromance clichés that don't match real life experience.

To reframe the narrative, we must normalize male emotional expression without parody or pity. It's not "cute" when a man opens up. It's *human.* It's not weak to need others. It's wise.

Courage also means initiating. Many men wait for friendship to happen organically, but deep friendship rarely does. It takes reaching out. Saying "Hey, I could use a talk," or "You want to grab lunch this week?" These are small acts of bravery. And they matter.

It also means risking *awkwardness.* Yes, trying to deepen a friendship can feel vulnerable. Yes, it might not always land. But the reward is worth the risk. And most men, when approached with sincerity, are relieved to find someone else is trying too.

Mentorship plays a role here, too. Older men modeling healthy friendships create ripple effects. So do emotionally intelligent men who make space for others. The more we see men loving each other platonically, supporting each other openly, and checking in regularly, the more we normalize it.

Rewriting the friendship narrative isn't just about emotional wellbeing. It's about redefining masculinity. It's about saying, *being a man doesn't mean going it alone. It means showing up with strength, yes, but also with heart.*

V. Building from Scratch: Tools, Tactics, and Real Life Application

So how do you actually build male friendships in adulthood especially if you're starting with few or none? The good news is it's possible at any age. The better news is it doesn't require being extroverted, emotionally fluent, or even particularly skilled at socializing. It just requires *intentionality* and *consistency.*

1. Start with Shared Interests

The fastest way to male friendship is mutual activity. Join a recreational sports league. Attend a meetup for a hobby. Take a class, volunteer, or show up at the same event regularly. These environments create natural shoulder to shoulder interaction, which lowers the pressure and creates a foundation for casual familiarity.

2. Look for the "Friendliness Spark"

Not every interaction has to lead to friendship but pay attention to the people you click with. Who makes you laugh? Who seems grounded? Who follows up with a question instead of a one word answer? These are your potential people.

3. Make the Move

Once you've spotted someone you vibe with, make the first move. It can be simple:

- "You free to grab a drink sometime?"
- "We should catch a game together one weekend."
- "What's your number? Let's keep in touch."

It may feel like asking someone out and in a way, it is. But remember: most guys are just waiting for someone to make the first gesture.

4. Create Rituals

Friendship doesn't sustain itself without rhythm. Set up recurring hangouts a biweekly poker night, Sunday hikes, or Tuesday gym sessions. Rituals provide structure and make the friendship part of your routine rather than another to-do item.

5. Be a Steady Presence

Show up. Not just physically, but emotionally. Ask about their life. Celebrate their wins. Remember the name of their kid or dog. These are the small signals that say, *I care.*

6. Let Yourself Be Seen

Vulnerability deepens friendship. Start small share a worry, talk about a challenge, admit a mistake. The goal isn't to trauma dump but to show you're human. When you open up, others often feel permission to do the same.

7. Give It Time

Friendships aren't microwavable. They take time to build, layer by layer. Don't panic if it feels slow. Keep showing up. Keep reaching out. Deep friendship isn't fast it's forged.

In Closing: Brotherhood is a Muscle Use It or Lose It

The code of brotherhood isn't broken. It's just hidden beneath layers of cultural baggage, emotional hesitation, and logistical noise. But when men take the time and the risk to build true friendships, they unlock something lifegiving.

This chapter isn't just about friendship. It's about reclaiming connection, vulnerability, and emotional strength. It's about rewriting what it means to be a man in community with other men. It's about building a tribe not of toughness and silence, but of trust and truth.

Because in the end, every man deserves someone to laugh with, cry with, grow with and walk shoulder to shoulder with through the mess and magic of life.

CHAPTER 14

Love Starts With You The Inner Work of a Good Partner

Have you ever found yourself wondering why relationships can be so challenging, even when love is present? Is there a secret to becoming a better partner, one that doesn't start with changing the other person but begins by looking within? These questions often surface when relationships hit rocky patches or when we realize past patterns repeating themselves in current interactions. It's easy to point fingers or believe that the grass might be greener elsewhere, but what if the key to unlocking healthier relationships lies in the work we do on ourselves?

This chapter will delve into the essential self-work necessary for cultivating meaningful relationships. Before offering love to someone else, it's crucial to develop self-awareness, emotional maturity, and inner stability. By understanding our behavioral tendencies, emotional triggers, and love languages, we can transform not only how we interact with partners but also how we view ourselves within the framework of love.

Know Yourself First

Understanding oneself plays a pivotal role in cultivating meaningful relationships. At the core of this journey is the awareness of your behavioral tendencies, emotional vulnerabilities, and preferred modes of affection, known as love languages. These self-discoveries form the groundwork for more profound connections with others. When you recognize your patterns, triggers, and emotional scars, you uncover the influence they wield on your interactions. Self-awareness, therefore, becomes the cornerstone upon which healthier and more genuine relationships thrive.

Self-reflection stands as an effective tool for expanding self-awareness. Start by identifying situations that provoke a strong emotional reaction. For instance, you might notice a particular situation where criticism, even when constructive, elicits defensiveness or anger. These reactions often point to an underlying unresolved issue or insecurity. Observing and noting these instances can unravel recurring patterns, especially during moments of conflict or stress. This exercise isn't just about recognizing the what but delving into the why. What is it about this scenario that strikes a nerve? As you explore these questions, you begin to map the connections between external stimuli and internal responses.

Recently, the concept of love languages has emerged as a significant component of relationship dynamics. Understanding your primary love language be it words of affirmation, acts of service, receiving gifts, quality time, or physical touch sheds light on how you express love and expect to receive it. Awareness of this can transform interactions, as it enhances your ability to communicate needs and appreciate gestures from others in the way they intend to convey love. When you understand how your love language aligns or conflicts with your partner's, you open doors for mutual comprehension and empathy.

Mapping emotional triggers is another critical aspect of self-discovery. Picture common scenarios that trigger strong emotional responses. List these triggers alongside past experiences that might have shaped them. Perhaps the tone of voice or a specific phrase used during an argument recalls memories of past relationships, thus eliciting a more intense reaction. By analyzing these connections, you gain insight into how these past experiences affect your current relationship dynamics.

To deepen the understanding, consider how these triggers specifically impact your interactions. Let's say a partner's abrupt departure during a disagreement resurrects feelings of abandonment from childhood. Noticing this connection provides an opportunity to discuss these emotions openly, paving the way for more supportive and understanding responses in future interactions. This emotional mapping encourages learning from past experiences without letting them dictate present interrelations.

The journey of self-discovery also involves addressing and healing old wounds. Reflect on unresolved issues that routinely affect your relationship, whether recurring insecurities or leftover resentment. Identify their origins and how they interfere with your emotional wellbeing today. Once you outline these factors, brainstorm strategies to address and heal these emotional scars. This might involve dialogues with your partner, professional counseling, or personal approaches such as journaling and mindfulness practices. The aim is to cultivate an environment where you can resolve these issues, freeing your present self from the burdens of past experiences.

Exploring these emotional scars in detail, consider how they influence your current mindset and behaviors towards partners. Embedded within emotional scars may lie unfounded beliefs or fears that coexist with your reality. For example, youth experiences with rejection might foster a belief that affection must always be earned, leading to constant reassurance, seeking behavior in relationships. Unpacking these associations and consciously challenging their validity creates room for healthier mental and emotional patterns to emerge.

The transformation that stems from understanding personal patterns and emotional frameworks holds value beyond romantic relationships. The same self-awareness and introspection extend to friendships, professional associations, and familial ties. The ripple effect of inner clarity and stability enhances broader social interactions, making the journey of self-discovery not just an investment in personal relationships, but in life as a whole.

While personal patterns and triggers often root themselves deeply in individual history, addressing them requires courage and honesty with oneself. Seeing these facilitative steps as part of a bigger picture helps. Debunking outdated societal norms and embracing emotional openness are concepts woven into this reflective tapestry. Understanding personal dynamics is a steppingstone to tackling more profound societal themes, such as challenging entrenched views of masculinity or valuing emotional expressiveness over stoicism.

The path to healing and self-discovery isn't devoid of challenges but embracing this journey equips you with the defenses to tackle those challenges. Engaging deeply in these exercises and methods reveals the emotional tapestry that forms your behavioral landscape. This unveiling ensures openness to growth in dimensions that enhance every relationship you value. Therefore, as you explore self-reflection, emotional mapping, and healing, the emergence from this journey promises deeper, more satisfying connections grounded in awareness and authenticity.

The Myth of the Stoic Man

In the previous section, we explored the importance of understanding your own patterns, triggers, wounds, and love languages. This self-awareness is crucial because it lays the foundation for tackling many outdated norms, particularly those related to masculinity that insist on stoicism as a virtue. When we say "stoic," we often refer to a kind of emotional unavailability that leaves no room for vulnerability or expression. However, understanding these personal dynamics allows men to challenge this notion and begin embracing emotional openness a necessary step for cultivating fulfilling relationships.

Much of what we've been taught about masculinity is based on myths. Historically, society has praised stoicism in men, equating emotional restraint with strength. This narrative not only hinders men from expressing their feelings but also limits their potential as partners. The myth of the stoic man suggests that showing emotion is a form of weakness. It suggests that asking for support or admitting vulnerability is somehow less masculine. Yet, this couldn't be further from the truth. Emotional openness doesn't mean displaying unchecked emotion; it means having the ability to express one's feelings and needs appropriately and to engage in deep, meaningful interactions.

One might wonder, why challenge this stoic archetype? Simply put, emotional openness leads to richer, more meaningful relationships. Consider this: a partner who can freely express emotions creates an environment where both parties feel seen and heard. This openness fosters a deeper connection, intimacy, and trust. Imagine a scenario where a man openly shares his fears and insecurities. His partner gains insight into his emotional world, creating room for empathy and understanding. As a result, both partners feel closer because they share a bond forged from genuine, heartfelt communication.

Another key aspect is emotional maturity, which is intertwined with self-awareness and inner stability. Emotional maturity means acknowledging and understanding one's emotions rather than suppressing them. It's about responding to your feelings in constructive ways. When a man moves past the myth of stoicism, he taps into the freedom that comes with fully participating in his emotional landscape. This doesn't just help in romantic relationships; it extends to friendships, family, and workplace dynamics. For example, think of a man who gets feedback at work that he initially perceives as critical. A stoic response might be to bottle up his feelings. An emotionally mature response involves processing those feelings, seeking clarification, and using the feedback constructively.

Men who embrace emotional openness often find personal satisfaction and relational success. When they are open, they encourage the same from others, creating cycles of positivity and trust. Take the simple act of saying, "I'm struggling today." This candidness can transform a simple day-to-day interaction into a deeply connecting moment. His partner then feels equally free to communicate similar feelings, thereby strengthening their emotional bond. These moments build a stable and supportive relationship where both individuals feel valued.

Breaking down the myth of stoicism involves understanding the full spectrum of human emotions. It's crucial to acknowledge that emotions are universal; they transcend gender. The ability to express emotions fluently enables men to live more authentically, aligning with their true selves. When emotional openness becomes a shared goal within a relationship, both partners contribute to a nurturing environment. This environment encourages growth and understanding, paving the way for resilient partnerships. Imagine a man who isn't afraid to cry at a sad movie or express joy openly. He sets a precedent that it's okay to feel deeply, offering a healthier model of masculinity for everyone around him.

This transformation requires dedication and ongoing self-reflection. As those ingrained ideas of masculinity shift, individuals must confront the weight of societal expectations. Embracing vulnerability isn't always easy, especially in cultures where stoicism has long been the standard. However, the rewards are immense. Vulnerability doesn't mean exposure to harm; instead, it brings the gift of deeper human connections. Friends, family, and partners are more likely to reciprocate openness and trust when a person shows his true emotions. The resulting relationships aren't defined by fear or superficial interactions but are deeply rooted in mutual respect and authenticity.

Consider the story of a father who resolves to embrace emotional transparency with his children. Instead of projecting a façade of unwavering strength, he shares tales of his own challenges and how he's navigated them. His children grow up knowing emotions are a natural, healthy aspect of human life. They learn to articulate their feelings without fear of judgment, developing emotional intelligence that will serve them well into adulthood.

As this chapter draws to a close, we turn toward the next crucial step: healing from the past. The acceptance of emotional openness inevitably leads to encountering past wounds we may have thought were long hidden. By addressing unresolved issues from childhood or previous relationships, one can recognize patterns that currently disrupt their ability to nurture healthy connections. It's crucial to acknowledge how these unresolved elements manifest in our behaviors and emotional reactions today. Perhaps an individual avoids confrontation because of early experiences with conflict. Recognizing this allows them to confront and dispel those fears.

The journey of self-improvement involves dismantling outdated myths about stoic masculinity and replacing them with healthy emotional practices. Awareness and willingness to change set the stage for authentic relationships. In moving forward, consider how past experiences shape your current interactions. Emotional openness becomes not just a tool for personal growth but a means to address lingering emotional baggage. This work allows individuals to step fully into their roles as loving, understanding partners who thrive on trust and emotional connection.

Healing the Past

Embracing emotional openness allows us to understand and address unresolved issues from our past, whether childhood experiences or lingering emotions from previous relationships. This understanding isn't just about facing discomfort. It's about creating a space where true healing can begin. Recognizing that our past shapes who we are today is the first step in transforming these insights into opportunities for growth. When we explore the depths of our emotions, we often uncover patterns that seem deeply ingrained.

Imagine a man who, as a child, experienced abandonment. This might manifest as fear of intimacy in his adult life, leading to commitment issues. Such experiences can influence our attachment styles, making some of us overly dependent or overly detached. Understanding these behavioral patterns sheds light on the ways they affect our adult relationships. Grasping how these wounds show up in our lives prepares us to address them. In diving into the roots of these feelings and experiences, we can begin to dismantle the walls they've built around us. We can start to rewrite the narrative, allowing us to approach life and love from a place of strength and authenticity.

Trying to build a loving relationship without first healing these past wounds can be like trying to build a house on an unstable foundation. Everything might look fine at first, but when tensions rise, the cracks begin to show. Addressing these issues fortifies our emotional foundation, preparing us to love others without clouded lenses or defensive barriers. Emotional readiness is all about knowing that we can enter relationships with a clear mind and a full heart, free from the shadows of our past. This kind of readiness leads to healthier interactions, marked by transparency, trust, and genuine connection.

Examining past trauma is crucial for understanding potential disruptions in trust within relationships. For instance, trust issues stemming from betrayal in a past relationship often make it difficult for someone to fully invest in new ones. It's as if there's an invisible wall preventing them from stepping into vulnerability. Healing these scars enables us to understand that not every new relationship carries the same fate as the old ones, allowing us to engage with others more openly. This examination demands honesty with ourselves. It's about recognizing that the fear of repeating past mistakes shouldn't prevent us from pursuing future possibilities.

Let's consider communication breakdowns in relationships, another area where past wounds manifest. Someone who grew up in an environment where feelings were dismissed might struggle to articulate emotions effectively. When you avoid addressing these communication barriers, misunderstandings become frequent, and resentment can quickly build. By healing past deprivations in communication, we develop better tools to express thoughts and feelings, promoting healthier dialogues with partners. This is not just about finding the right words. It's about learning to listen and speak in ways that resonate authentically, fostering mutual understanding and compassion.

Healing isn't instant. It's a process that requires patience and persistence. It calls for acknowledging pain, experiencing it fully, and letting it go. This journey of self-improvement demands introspection and sometimes the courage to ask for help. Therapy, self-reflection, and even conversations with trusted loved ones can provide invaluable insights into our emotional landscapes. By doing this inner work, we break free from the chains of our past, making room for a new era of relational engagement. Stepping away from patterns shaped by old wounds allows us to forge new paths filled with possibility.

Additionally, the interplay between past experiences and current relationships includes understanding how ingrained reactions can jeopardize present interactions. A person who faced criticism in their formative years might react defensively to feedback from a partner. This isn't just about being sensitive; it's about learning to differentiate between constructive criticism and personal attacks. Healing past experiences helps differentiate between present realities and shadows of bygone days. This understanding fosters environments where partners feel appreciated and understood for who they truly are, resulting in a stronger bond.

Further exploration reveals that past traumas can shape expectations in relationships. For example, if one grew up in an environment where affection was conditional, they might anticipate similar conditions in current relationships. The expectation shaped by past experiences can create a constant tension, perpetuating a cycle of insecurity and doubt. Healing these past wounds empowers us to establish relationship expectations grounded in mutual respect, inspiration, and unconditional support. This is a shift from fear based love to love that is genuine and brave, creating space for authentic connections.

As we heal and grow, we realize the importance of self-awareness and its impact on our relationships. Self-awareness bridges the past and the present, helping us understand how former experiences shape current dynamics. This insight allows us to empathize with others, making us more compassionate partners. Our ability to step into our partners' shoes translates to deeper, more meaningful connections. Through this understanding, we create spaces that nurture growth, not confinement.

In examining how understanding past experiences contribute to personal growth, recognizing their influence on relational engagements becomes pivotal. Relationships transform from stagnant to thriving when healing the past is prioritized. We engage with others through the lens of clarity, absent of misconceptions bred by unresolved emotions. This transformation enriches the relationship, enhancing emotional connection and engagement, and facilitates the development of healthier patterns.

As we wrap up this exploration of healing, it transitions seamlessly into discussing "The Power of Presence" in relationships. Healing past wounds is fundamental in developing this presence. It lets us fully engage with others in the present, not distracted by unresolved issues or lingering doubts from our past experiences. This liberated engagement enables us to be genuinely there for those we love, and it enhances our relational bonds in profound ways. Once we shed the ghostly chains of past wounds, we pave the way for deepening connections grounded in authenticity and true presence.

The Power of Presence

Unresolved issues from childhood or past relationships often haunt our present. They infringe upon our ability to fully engage with others, clouding our interactions with unaddressed fears and pain. When these specters linger, they rob us of the capacity to remain present and emotionally attuned. This absence of presence can sway the dynamics of our relationships, making them turbulent and disconnected. The power of presence, therefore, emerges not as a novelty but a necessity for meaningful connection.

Being fully present involves more than the physical act of showing up. It requires emotional engagement and mental clarity, anchoring us in the moment with our partner. When we're present, we're attentive to our partner's needs and tuned into the nuances of interaction that might otherwise go unnoticed. It's less about saying all the right things or orchestrating grand gestures, and more about making each moment matter.

Consider the difference between two people: One relies on extravagant gifts to express affection, while the other invests in quiet, quality time with their partner. The former might impress initially, but it's often the latter who forms a more profound connection. The investment of presence fosters security and emotional resonance that outlasts superficial displays.

Presence acts as a soil wherein trust and intimacy can grow. When you're truly present, you notice subtle changes in your partner's mood, or the fine lines of stress etched across their forehead. You become adept at listening, not just hearing, allowing exploration of thoughts and feelings that might otherwise remain buried. In this space, empathy flourishes, enabling you to respond with genuine understanding rather than defaulting to knee-jerk reactions driven by your own emotional baggage.

Self-awareness forms the foundational skill essential for cultivating presence. When you embark on a sincere journey of self-reflection, you recognize your emotions and behaviors while understanding how they affect your relationship dynamics. This knowledge becomes a powerful tool in managing conflicts and enhancing communication. With self-awareness, you're less likely to project unhealed wounds onto your partner, and more likely to hold space for both of you.

Emotional engagement is about being involved in your emotional life with intentionality and consciousness. Instead of shying away from vulnerability, embrace it. When you do, you invite your partner to do the same. Spiraling inward, emotional engagement means harmonizing your emotional rhythms with those of your partner. You learn to dance along the lines of joy and sorrow, weaving a fabric from life's varied textures.

In everyday interactions, presence shines brightly. Imagine an evening spent with your partner after a long day. You could easily retreat into your world of thoughts, scroll through social media, or half listen to their recounting of the day. But instead, you choose presence. You put your phone away, focus, and delve into their world. This small decision to be fully with them transforms a mundane evening into a cherished memory.

The distinction is stark between someone who genuinely embodies presence and one who leans on superficial gestures. The latter might buy a bouquet a day after forgetting an anniversary, while the former remembers a small detail from weeks ago, bringing it up in conversation deliberately to show they've been listening. Presence is continual and consistent, a muscle flexed not only in grand gestures but in the quiet constancy of each interaction.

This approach doesn't just enrich the relationship, but nurtures emotional maturity. By choosing to be present, you prioritize partnership over self-centric tendencies. It's a practice that says, "You matter to me, and because you do, I am here to truly experience you." Presence becomes a cornerstone of emotional intelligence, underpinning every interaction with grace and mindfulness.

As you begin to cultivate presence, you'll notice a natural shift: Relationships built on this foundation exhibit resilience. Presence breeds a level of trust that makes navigating conflicts less daunting. When secure in your presence, your partner is less likely to feel threatened by disagreements and more open to collaborative solutions.

Presence naturally leads us toward other virtuous qualities. As you learn to be actively present, you inherently start building characteristics like reliability, accountability, and kindness character qualities vital for any thriving relationship. These qualities become romantic superpowers, fortifying the bedrock upon which relationships thrive. Reliable presence reassures your partner that they can count on you; accountability ensures that you own your actions in the relationship; kindness makes an environment where both people feel cherished and valued.

In developing genuine presence, you prepare the ground for these superpowers to flourish, igniting a cycle where each quality enriches the other. Presence invites reliability, as being there consistently builds trust over time. Accountability grows under the umbrella of presence, enabling us to own up gracefully to our shortcomings and commitments. Kindness, always close at heart, becomes the language through which presence is expressed.

Now, as we move forward, we'll delve into how we can cultivate habitual reliability, accountability, and kindness. These aren't just mere virtues but acts that enhance the presence you've already embraced. Through the continuous practice of these qualities, you not only deepen the bond with your partner but also evolve within yourself, making the inner work of love a journey, not a destination. As the seed of presence grows into the tree of relational strength, the roots of these habits keep it grounded and thriving.

Character Over Charm

Picture this: You're truly present in your relationships, listening with intention and authenticity because you understand that being emotionally available outweighs any grand gesture you could ever make. That's the essence of what we've been exploring in previous chapters. Now, let's dive into the inner habits that can transform you into a partner whose love feels like a superpower habits like reliability, accountability, and kindness.

Being reliable is more powerful than you might think. It's about showing up when you say you will not just physically, but mentally and emotionally too. Think about it. When you commit to a plan or promise, and then keep it, you convey to your partner that they can trust you to be there. This consistent behavior creates an environment of stability and trust, which is incredibly attractive. Perhaps it's about remembering to pick up groceries or simply calling at a time you both agreed. These habits seem small, but each act is a brick in the growing wall of trust you and your partner build together.

But how do you enhance reliability in daily life? Start by creating a habit of double checking your calendar for commitments you've made and then noting them in a way you won't forget. Use digital reminders or a planner whatever you're most likely to check regularly. Your commitment to reminders demonstrates reliability in action.

Steps to enhance reliability:

1. Review all your commitments for the upcoming week every Sunday evening.
2. Set reminders on your phone for each task and event.
3. Be honest about your capability to take on commitments. If it's too much, communicate it early.

4. At the end of each day, note which tasks you completed and which ones you didn't. Consider what blocked your success.

Accountability is the next cornerstone. It fosters respect in relationships, showing you can own up to mistakes and learn from them. Being accountable isn't always easy; it requires humility and bravery. But imagine the trust you earn when you admit, "I didn't handle that well. Here's what I'll do differently next time." This statement alone can open doors to resolution and growth.

To foster accountability in your interactions:

1. Recognize when a situation hasn't gone as planned.

2. Reflect on your role in the outcome. Assess both your actions and words.

3. Communicate with your partner by acknowledging your role and suggest a realistic way to prevent it in the future.

4. Follow through with your proposed change.

By incorporating accountability into your relationships, you become someone who your partner can respect, not just love. This respect is crucial for maintaining a healthy dynamic, especially when disagreements arise.

Next, consider the power of kindness. Kindness nurtures connection by keeping relationships alive with acts that come from a genuine place of caring. It's often the soft words or shared laughter during mundane moments that become a couple's cherished memories. This gentle superpower is about active listening, offering words of encouragement, and doing little acts of love not because you gain from it, but because it strengthens your bond.

To cultivate kindness as a habit:

1. Begin each day with an intention for kindness. It could be as simple as, "I will listen fully when spoken to."

2. Focus on meaningful compliments acknowledge the small things you value about your partner.

3. Schedule an act of kindness weekly, like preparing their favorite meal or writing a note.

4. Reflect on your actions weekly. Ask yourself how you felt giving and what you observed receiving.

In your journey of self-awareness, emotional maturity, and inner stability, these habits become powerful tools. They're not one time actions but ongoing processes that drive personal growth impacting how you give and receive love. As these habits weave into your everyday life, you'll notice they don't just help in romantic relationships, but transform your connections in general, making you a more empathetic and understanding person.

Think about reliability, and how your friends start valuing your dependability. Consider accountability and how your colleagues might appreciate your ownership and proactive problem-solving. Reflect on kindness and how it might make strangers smile and friends feel seen. These qualities were always within you, waiting to be nurtured and expressed in every relationship you care about.

Incorporating these traits into the fabric of your daily life involves patience and consistency. Remember that growing into a better version of yourself is a lifelong journey. Each step you take towards cultivating these romantic superpowers makes you not just a better partner but a better man. As you reflect on these practices, keep exploring how they feel and fit into various aspects of your life. How do they shape your work, friendships, and the way you interact with the world?

Your relationships are a reflection of the love you invest in yourself. When you're reliable, you're not just showing up for someone else you're showing up for you. When you're accountable, you not only gain respect from others but also integrity within yourself. Every act of kindness you extend finds its way back to you, often when you least expect it. Explore these habits, and watch as they unfold the kind of relationship you've always wanted grounded, honest, and full of respect and love.

Takeaways

Having explored the foundational aspects of self-awareness, emotional maturity, and relational stability in this chapter, we now recognize that becoming a better man in love begins with enriching our understanding of ourselves. By embracing self-reflection to uncover patterns and triggers, we lay the groundwork for healthier interactions. This exploration of love languages and emotional scars reveals how past experiences influence our present relationships, urging us to challenge outdated norms of masculinity that equate stoicism with strength. As we move forward, we can harness these insights to cultivate richer, more genuine connections. With a commitment to emotional openness, we unravel the myths that have constrained us, paving the way for authentic partnerships rooted in empathy and mutual respect. The journey of self-discovery doesn't just prepare us to give love meaningfully; it transforms every facet of our lives, empowering us to become individuals capable of nurturing deep, satisfying bonds with those we cherish.

The Art of Romance; How to Connect, Communicate, & Create Intimacy

Have you ever wondered why some relationships seem to thrive effortlessly, while others struggle to maintain their spark? Couples often find themselves lost in the daily grind, leaving little time for the small acts of love that truly matter. What is it that keeps emotional and physical intimacy alive, while some partners drift apart without even realizing it? Could there be a key to unlocking deeper connections and more meaningful communication?

This chapter delves into the art of romance by exploring how intentional acts can nurture and strengthen relationships over time. We'll examine the nuances of connecting with your partner through everyday gestures, clear communication, and shared experiences. By understanding how to incorporate these elements into daily life, you'll discover ways to maintain a fulfilling partnership filled with warmth and intimacy.

Romance is in the Details, Keeping the Spark Alive

In the whirlwind of daily life, it's easy to overlook the small yet significant acts that can deeply nurture a romantic relationship. We often hear the phrase "It's the little things that count," and this rings especially true when it comes to maintaining a strong and loving bond with our partners. While grand gestures are memorable and exciting, it's the everyday moments that steadily build a foundation of love and trust.

Consider a tender touch. A simple gesture such as holding hands or offering a comforting hug can speak volumes about connection. These small acts of affection are essential, as they communicate warmth and love without needing words. When partners acknowledge each other's presence with a gentle touch after a long day, it signals, "I see you, and I'm here." This physical reminder of affection helps to maintain an emotional closeness that supports building a lasting relationship.

Similarly, the power of a thoughtful note can't be overstated. Imagine opening your lunch to find a sticky note that reads, "Thinking of you, hope your day is wonderful!" Such surprises can instantly lift spirits and reinforce feelings of being cherished. When partners take the time to express their thoughts through written words, they provide reassurance and connection. A thoughtful note is a physical reminder that someone cares enough to take that little extra step.

Then there's the impact of an unexpected kind word. Compliments and words of encouragement foster positive emotional environments. Saying, "You handled that situation wonderfully," or "I appreciate everything you do for us," showcases gratitude and appreciation. These verbal affirmations remind partners that their efforts are seen and valued, strengthening mutual esteem and respect.

Attention to detail often manifests through consistent date nights. As many relationships develop, the intentionality around spending quality time together might decline. Yet reserving a regular evening devoted to one another helps maintain romance and excitement. Date nights infuse the mundane routine with novelty and adventure, offering opportunities to connect, laugh, and share stories. Whether it's trying a new restaurant, attending a class together, or staying in for a cozy movie night, it's the commitment to these moments that underline their importance.

Impromptu adventures offer another avenue for deepening intimacy. When spontaneity enters a relationship, it breaks monotony and initiates a sense of freedom and wonder. Surprising your partner with a weekend getaway or suggesting an unplanned hike creates shared experiences and memories. These spur-of-the-moment choices enable partners to explore their yearning to share life's beautiful and unpredictable moments together, thus strengthening partnership.

Shared hobbies present yet another powerful tool in relationship enhancement. Engaging in mutual interests allows partners to unwind and bond over a common passion. Whether it's gardening, cooking, or going on cycling trips, shared activities promote teamwork and communication. These shared experiences create a safe space where partners can express themselves openly, further fostering that essential emotional connection.

All these small actions cumulatively enrich relationships by signaling consideration and effort. They reflect a deep attentiveness to the partner's needs and desires, enhancing the fabric of the relationship. These acts may appear minor, but their impact is profound because they demonstrate ongoing dedication and love.

Communication serves as the backbone of these actions. Listening without defensiveness allows both partners to feel heard and respected. It's about understanding rather than responding, creating a dialogue where partners can share openly and honestly. Speaking with clarity helps ensure that conversations are constructive rather than confusing. It implies being direct with feelings and thoughts, reducing the chances of misunderstanding and friction.

Expressing needs without blame is crucial. When articulating desires or concerns, it's important to focus on one's feelings rather than blaming a partner. This approach fosters a nurturing environment where both individuals feel valued and respected. Expressing needs sensitively paves the way for positive, solution oriented exchanges.

As these areas of communication intertwine with daily gestures of love and care, they reinforce the romantic atmosphere in the relationship. By ensuring both partners are emotionally aligned, the loving actions gain deeper meanings and become more impactful. This emphasis on communication acts as a bridge, allowing partners to continuously grow and adapt together.

Thus, meaningful relationships stem from weaving intentional actions into everyday life. Embracing the little things, from affectionate gestures to shared activities, cultivates a shared experience full of understanding and warmth. With effective communication as the anchor, partners can navigate their relationship journey with mutual love, respect, and joy. Through this dance of tender gestures and heartfelt conversations, they create a lasting and fulfilling connection.

Communicate Like You Care

In the previous section, we touched on how small gestures can profoundly impact relationships, far beyond grand displays of affection. Now let's focus on how communication serves as the foundation for these everyday acts of love. When you think about it, even a single word or lack thereof can steer the course of your relationship. A casual "How was your day?" can open avenues for connection, while a dismissive tone can quickly erode trust and closeness.

Effective communication within romantic relationships is crucial, and it involves much more than merely talking. Listening without defensiveness, speaking with clarity, and expressing needs constructively all contribute to meaningful dialogue. Each of these skills requires intention and practice but pays off when applied consistently.

Listening without defensiveness can be a gamechanger. When your partner shares something with you, especially if it involves criticism or a request, it's natural to feel the urge to defend yourself. However, reacting defensively can shut down communication and build walls rather than bridges. Instead, practice active listening. Nod to show you're engaged. Summarize what your partner has said to confirm understanding. "So, you're feeling overwhelmed because of my late work hours?" This technique not only shows that you've heard them but also paves the way for empathy. A simple gesture like maintaining eye contact during these exchanges signals that you care and are fully present.

Empathy plays a critical role here. Putting yourself in your partner's shoes helps you understand things from their perspective, defusing potential conflicts before they flare up. Say your partner feels neglected due to your busy schedule. By empathizing, you might reflect, "If I imagined myself in their place, I'd feel ignored too." Acknowledging their feelings doesn't mean you agree completely, but it opens up space for a more productive conversation.

Speaking with clarity is equally vital. Relationships often involve discussions that evoke strong emotions. Keeping a cool head and communicating clearly can make all the difference. Practice calm articulation by pausing and gathering your thoughts before speaking, especially if you're in a heated moment. "What exactly bothers me?" or "How can I express this without escalating the tension?" Also, use "I" statements to own your feelings and avoid placing blame. "I feel hurt when plans change abruptly" comes off much less accusatory than "You always change plans at the last minute."

Moreover, conveying emotions clearly gets easier with practice and understanding your communication style. Whether you are more straightforward or indirect, knowing your tendencies can help tailor your approach. A straightforward communicator might need to work on softening their delivery, while a more subtle individual might need to emphasize clarity. This self-awareness allows for better conversations.

Expressing needs without blame is perhaps the trickiest yet most rewarding. Ensuring your needs are met without pointing fingers requires tact and kindness. A helpful framework is to articulate what you feel, what you need, and how your partner can help. Suppose you feel unseen in your relationship; instead of saying "You never pay attention to me," opt for "I feel a lack of presence from us lately, and I crave more quality time together." This approach not only clarifies your desire but also invites your partner to collaborate on a solution rather than feel cornered.

Miscommunications often stem from assumptions. We assume our partners know what we want or how we feel, which isn't always the case. Be explicit about your needs and expectations. Sometimes saying, "I need you to listen right now rather than offer solutions," can transform an entire conversation. Similarly, ensure the focus remains on what you want to resolve rather than who's at fault. Constructive communication strengthens the partnership because it shows both parties are invested in success.

These communication strategies seamlessly set the stage for the next aspect of relational growth: emotional intelligence. Mastering effective communication allows you to employ emotional intelligence more proficiently. It enhances your ability to read between the lines, interpret nonverbal cues, and ask questions that delve deeper into the emotional undercurrents of your relationship. Advanced communication skills enable you to discern what isn't being said, often the key to discovering what truly plagues a relationship.

For instance, if your partner seems distant, asking insightful questions could uncover stressors from their day that impacted their mood. "Did something happen at work today?" or "Is there anything else on your mind that we haven't talked about?" These questions not only show concern but also demonstrate a proactive step toward understanding and resolving potential disputes before they escalate.

Your relationship will thrive on this mutual understanding as it lays the groundwork for a harmonious and fulfilling partnership. By building on these foundational communication tools, you and your partner can navigate the nuances of emotional conversations with grace and resilience. This equips you both with the awareness needed to foster a more profound connection, where every interaction, big or small, is steeped in the care that nurtures a lasting relationship.

Understanding Her Needs (Without Reading Her Mind)

In the prior discussion, we touched upon listening without falling into defensiveness, speaking with a clear voice, and expressing needs without blame. These principles lay the groundwork for understanding how emotional intelligence breathes life into a relationship. It's about closing the gap between you and your partner by being attuned to their needs and feelings. Recognizing your partner's needs demands more than just good intentions; it requires the artful application of emotional intelligence. Let's explore how to put this into action.

You find that emotional intelligence in relationships centers on asking thoughtful questions and paying attention to your partner's responses both verbal and nonverbal. For instance, if you're picking up on body language indicating stress or anxiety but the words being said are, "I'm fine," it's time to dig deeper. A simple yet effective question you might ask is, "What can I do to support you right now?" This not only opens the floor for your partner to express their feelings more authentically but also conveys that you care about their wellbeing.

Understanding these cues enhances your ability to address the unspoken needs. Maybe your partner has had a tough day, and what they truly need is a comforting presence rather than a barrage of solutions or advice. By asking the right questions and listening deeply, you validate their feelings and show that their emotional state is valuable to you. This, in turn, builds trust and openness.

Seeing emotional intelligence in action is about noticing those little details. Consider a partner who often dismisses their own feelings, shrugging off emotional distress with phrases like, "It is what it is." Recognizing this as a defense mechanism might prompt you to offer reassurance or to remind them that expressing emotions is not a sign of weakness. The ability to consistently show thoughtfulness, by acknowledging their struggles and providing a safe space for sharing feelings, demonstrates a high level of emotional understanding and encourages genuine communication.

Another example might be realizing that your partner feels overwhelmed during social gatherings but struggles to express it directly. Observing their discomfort, you could take the initiative to offer alternative plans for a quieter evening. This highlights how small acts of empathy can prevent misunderstandings and foster closeness.

When we talk about asking insightful questions, it's essential to focus on open-ended questions that encourage further conversation. For instance, instead of "Did you have a good day?" you might ask, "What was the highlight of your day?" This opens the door for your partner to reflect more deeply and share more about their experiences and emotions. Engaging in this kind of dialogue frequently creates a more supportive and connected partnership.

Emotional intelligence also includes knowing when to step back and give your partner space. It is a balancing act of being there when needed and respecting boundaries when your partner requires solitude. Recognizing this need for space and not taking it personally can be an important aspect of understanding and emotional intelligence.

It is equally important to resist making assumptions about your partner's feelings or reactions. Often, we might believe that we know our partner so well that we assume we know their needs without asking. However, presuming without checking in can lead to miscommunications and resentment. Keeping dialogue open and avoiding assumptions nurtures a shared understanding.

Once misunderstandings occur, having the emotional intelligence to manage and resolve conflicts calmly is essential. Instead of escalating, calmly expressing your perspective and giving your partner space to do the same underscores a mutual respect at the core of emotional intelligence. You acknowledge that it is not about who wins the argument but about finding common ground. This skill not only restores harmony quicker but also deepens your emotional connection.

Reflecting on skills like active listening and empathy enriches your emotional toolkit, making it easier to recognize your partner's verbal and nonverbal cues. Being tuned into these signals helps you respond authentically, elevating both conversation and interaction. Moreover, when you demonstrate a willingness to understand and address emotional cues, you foster a relationship environment where both partners are encouraged to develop and express emotional intelligence.

As you hone this skill set, you set the groundwork for a more balanced intimacy. Recognizing and addressing your partner's needs becomes second nature. This opens the pathway for the next stage, which harmoniously integrates emotional closeness with physical affection and sexual connection, culminating in a balanced and nurturing relationship.

Emotional intelligence forms the backbone of how we relate to each other, transforming routine conversations into opportunities for deeper connection and understanding. As we recognize the importance of empathy, active listening, and thoughtful engagement, we set a solid base upon which we can construct sustained intimacy. Understanding that every interaction has the potential to enrich our partnership, we pave the way toward a warm, considerate, and intimately connected relationship.

Looking ahead, we'll examine how emotional closeness intertwines with the physical realm, discovering the seamless tapestry they create when harmonized. This exploration highlights how emotional intelligence primes us for richer, more meaningful connections, both emotionally and physically. The balance of these elements is the beating heart of lasting intimacy, ensuring that love not only survives but thrives long after the first spark.

The Intimacy Equation

Building upon the foundation of emotional intelligence, intimate relationships flourish when partners can perceive and navigate emotional landscapes effectively. Emotional intelligence involves the ability to ask insightful questions, pick up on unspoken cues, and respond in ways that resonate with a partner's needs and preferences. It's not just about knowing what questions to ask, but also about listening actively and empathetically to the answers. This creates a cycle of understanding and trust that lays the groundwork for deeper connections.

Imagine a couple where one partner comes home visibly upset. Through the practice of emotional intelligence, the other partner notices subtle changes in their demeanor and offers a safe space for sharing by asking, "Do you want to talk about what's on your mind, or should we do something to distract ourselves for a while?" This simple act demonstrates an understanding of emotional needs, allowing the upset partner to feel seen and valued. The ability to navigate these moments with sensitivity can reinforce emotional closeness, which is one component of a successful relationship.

Beyond emotions, physical affection is another crucial dimension to consider. It's one of the most visible forms of connection hugs, kisses, holding hands, and even the warm glance across a room all contribute to a sense of closeness. Physical affection offers comfort, reinforces bonds, and provides a sense of security. For instance, a couple might develop a ritual of a comforting hug every morning before work, starting the day on a loving note. Such gestures are powerful; they bridge gaps without the need for words and tend to cultivate an atmosphere of mutual reassurance and care.

In addition to emotional and physical care, sexual connection holds significant importance in maintaining intimacy. Open and honest conversations about desires, boundaries, and preferences enrich this facet of a relationship. Exploring each other's needs should be a journey of shared discovery. When partners are in tune with each other's physical desires, it speaks volumes about their willingness to keep the wonder and allure alive. Imagine an evening where partners sit down and express curiosity about each other's fantasies, creating a deeper level of vulnerability and trust.

This not only spices up the relationship but also strengthens emotional and physical ties.

Focusing on these elements individually is not enough, though. The true art of romance lies in balancing these aspects harmoniously. Neglecting one could lead to dissatisfaction, while overemphasizing another might result in an imbalance that undermines overall intimacy. Successfully intertwining these strands requires ongoing dialogue and a willingness to adapt as the relationship evolves over time. This balance becomes a dance, with each partner willing to lead and follow in turn, maintaining grace and harmony in the relationship.

Consider a couple celebrating their tenth anniversary. Over the years, they maintain a steady flow of communication, consistently checking in with each other's emotional states. They've instituted regular date nights to keep the romantic spark alive, but they also value quiet evenings focused on conversation or shared hobbies. Maintaining a balance, they plan weekends away to ensure that time for physical and sexual closeness is prioritized amidst the bustle of daily life. This thoughtful approach helps them stay connected and fulfilled.

For relationships to thrive, this equilibrium requires flexibility. Life changes whether they be career shifts, growing families, or health challenges necessitate shifts in how couples manage their emotional, physical, and sexual connections. Understanding that change is inevitable, and embracing it with open dialogue and creative solutions, is key. Partners committed to adaptation find that their relationship not only survives but often becomes more resilient through challenges.

Another aspect to consider is how each person's background and previous experiences influence their perception of intimacy. Some may have learned that emotional expression is a sign of weakness, while others might equate physical touch with care.

Recognizing these differences allows each partner to explain and understand their position better, fostering an environment where vulnerability is welcomed rather than shunned. This understanding encourages both to share openly, deepening their bond.

Remember that healthy relationships aren't just born from grand gestures, but rather through consistent, small acts of love and attention. These everyday actions are opportunities to articulate love tangibly. A gentle reminder of support through a text, a thoughtful act like making coffee in the morning, or a spontaneous display of affection sparks connection throughout the day. These gestures accumulate over time, weaving a fabric of intimacy that withstands trials.

Conversely, missteps in managing this balance often lead to misunderstandings or conflict. Miscommunication or misinterpretation can quickly erode trust and affection. Therefore, couples should appreciate the importance of saying "I'm sorry" and understanding that forgiving is as crucial as asking for forgiveness. Resolving such conflicts can either tug partners apart or tighten the threads of their relationship, depending on their approach.

Ultimately, achieving the artful balance of emotional closeness, physical affection, and sexual connection requires effort, conscious choices, and willingness to evolve. It's an ongoing process involving negotiation, introspection, and sincerity, which, when attentively managed, leads to profound enrichment in relationships. The reward is a relationship resilient enough to navigate storms yet tender enough to revel in life's simple joys.

By being mindful of this delicate dance, partners not only sustain love, but nurture a relationship that grows richer with each passing year. They create a sanctuary where both feel cherished, understood, and inspired, forging a partnership that celebrates both individuality and unity.

Summary

As we have explored, the everyday acts of love and effective communication are crucial to maintaining a vibrant and enduring romantic relationship. Now that we understand the power of these small gestures like tender touches, thoughtful notes, and kind words and their impact on emotional and physical intimacy, we can intentionally incorporate them into our daily lives. By doing so, couples can foster an environment where both partners feel valued and connected. Moving forward, embracing open communication and empathy while nurturing these gestures will help ensure relationships not only survive but thrive. As partners continue this intentional dance of love and understanding, they create a resilient bond enriched with mutual respect and joy, paving the way for a future filled with shared happiness and fulfillment.

CHAPTER 16

Building a Love That Lasts. Marriage, Commitment, and Weathering the Storms

Marriage isn't just about the wedding day, the pretty photos, or even those "good morning" kisses though those are lovely perks. It's about what happens when the music fades, when life gets loud, and when love isn't convenient or cute. This chapter is a deep dive into what it really takes to build a love that lasts not for a season, but for a lifetime.

Whether you're newly married, many years in, or thinking about taking that leap someday, the truth is this: Marriage is not a finish line. It's the beginning of one long, winding, beautiful, messy journey. Let's walk through the map together.

Marriage as a Daily Choice

Let's bust one of the biggest myths about marriage: that it's all about feelings. The butterflies. The chemistry. The "can't-stop-thinking-about-you" romance. While that's part of it, feelings are notoriously unreliable. Some days, you'll feel madly in love. Other days, you'll feel mad full stop.

Love that lasts isn't powered by emotion alone. It's a *decision*. Every. Single. Day.

Choosing to stay when it's easier to walk away. Choosing to listen when you'd rather win the argument. Choosing to see your partner's strengths when their flaws are louder. That's love in action.

Think of love like a garden. Feelings are the flowers you notice them when they bloom. But the real work is in the soil. It's in the watering, the weeding, the patience. You show up even on the days it doesn't look pretty. That's the difference between infatuation and commitment.

Daily Commitment Checklist:

- Did I assume the best about my partner today?
- Did I speak to them with kindness even when stressed?
- Did I support their goals as much as my own?
- Did I choose patience over perfection?

Marriage doesn't thrive on autopilot. It takes active love consistent, intentional, and humble.

How to Fight Fair

No marriage is conflict free and that's a good thing. Disagreements mean you both care, think, and feel deeply. But the *way* you fight can make or break the health of your relationship.

Let's talk about *fighting fair* because arguments don't have to be ugly to be honest.

The Ground Rules of Respectful Conflict:

1. **Stay on Topic.** Don't drag in past fights or offload five different grievances at once.

2. **Don't Weaponize Words.** Avoid character attacks like "You always..." or "You never..." They're rarely true and instantly defensive.

3. **Take Timeouts.** If tempers rise, call a pause before damage is done. Come back when both are calm.

4. **Use "I" Statements.** Say, "I feel hurt when..." instead of "You're so selfish."

5. **Repair Matters More Than Being Right.** Be quicker to extend an olive branch than a smug "I told you so."

Healthy couples aren't those who never argue. They're the ones who know how to *reconnect* after a clash. They apologize. They reflect. They make adjustments. They don't use silence as punishment or love as leverage.

Fighting fair is not about avoiding hard conversations. It's about learning to disagree with honor, not hostility.

Respect, Loyalty, and Trust

If love is the heart of a marriage, trust is its backbone. And respect? That's the daily heartbeat. Let's look at these three together:

1. Respect

Respect means honoring your partner's dignity especially when you're frustrated or disappointed. It's speaking to them like a teammate, not a rival. It's not interrupting. It's not belittling them in front of others (or behind their back). It's recognizing their strengths and contributions, and saying *thank you* not out of obligation, but appreciation.

2. Loyalty

Loyalty is deeper than just "not cheating." It's emotional fidelity. Do you protect your spouse's reputation when they're not in the room? Do you vent to friends in a way that poisons your view of them? Do you mentally check out when life gets hard?

Loyalty shows up in the micro moments: defending their name, upholding their trust, and sticking by their side even when the world's against them.

3. Trust

Trust doesn't build itself. It's built brick by brick, through transparency, follow-through, and emotional availability. It grows when you:

- Keep your word.

- Share your feelings, not just facts.

- Handle your partner's vulnerabilities with care, not criticism.

- Apologize when you screw up and change the behavior that broke the trust.

When trust is strong, marriage becomes a sanctuary. When it breaks, everything feels unstable. The good news? Trust can be rebuilt. Slowly. Steadily. Through repeated integrity.

Growing Together, Not Apart

People change. Life changes. Seasons shift. The couple you were at 25 won't be the couple you are at 45 and that's not a flaw. It's a feature.

The secret is to grow together, not apart.

So many couples wake up one day and say, "Who are you?" But that's often because they stopped checking in. They stopped dating. They stopped dreaming together.

Ways to Stay Emotionally Aligned:

- Date nights aren't a luxury they're a lifeline. Make space to laugh, flirt, and play again.

- **Vision board as a couple.** Where do you both want to be in five years? Ten? Dream aloud together.

- **Keep learning about each other.** Ask deep questions. Explore new experiences. Don't assume you already know it all.

- **Celebrate wins, even small ones.** From career moves to emotional breakthroughs, affirm growth on both sides.

- **Support each other's individual passions.** Personal growth doesn't compete with partnership it fuels it.

Change is inevitable. Disconnection isn't. Stay curious about your partner as they evolve and let them do the same for you.

Being Her Safe Place

"Being the provider" has long been tied to financial security but that's only part of the picture. A true partner offers emotional security, too.

Being her safe place means:

- She can cry without judgment.

- She can share her fears without being fixed.

- She can mess up and still feel loved.

- She can speak up and be heard.

It also means creating a home environment that feels safe, not just physically but emotionally and psychologically. That might look like:

- Handling disagreements with calm instead of rage.

- Being consistent instead of unpredictable.

- Listening more than lecturing.

- Being her advocate, not her adversary.

A woman's heart opens widest when she feels safe not just sexually or physically, but *soul deep*. That safety? That's sacred.

Likewise, men deserve to be safe, too. Emotionally available. Fully seen. Vulnerability isn't a weakness, it's where connection lives.

Legacy of Love

Let's zoom out.

Beyond bills, date nights, and disagreements, your marriage tells a story. Every day, you're writing a legacy not just for yourselves, but for the people watching.

Your kids? They're learning what love looks like from how you handle stress, celebrate each other, and speak behind closed doors.

Your friends? They're being shaped by the marriage culture you contribute to whether that's full of cynicism or hope.

The world? It's hungry for examples of real, enduring love that weathers storms and still holds hands.

So, ask yourself:

- What kind of marriage would I want my children to mirror?

- What do I want to be remembered for as a partner?

- What impact does my relationship have on others?

Building a love that lasts means building something bigger than yourself. It's legacy work. It's soul work. And it's the kind of work that changes generations.

Final Reflections: Love Isn't Perfect But It's Worth It

Here's the truth: Some days, you won't like your spouse. You'll feel frustrated. Unheard. Exhausted. That doesn't mean your marriage is broken it means it's real.

Strong marriages aren't marked by perfection. They're marked by *repair.*

They're forged in moments when one person says, "I'm sorry," and the other says, "I forgive you."

They're built in the quiet acts making coffee, folding laundry, texting "Thinking of you."

They thrive in the unexpected laughter, the inside jokes, and the deep sighs of "I've got you, no matter what."

Marriage is hard. But when it's built with humility, resilience, and deep-rooted commitment it's also holy. It's healing. It's home.

So, keep choosing each other. Not just when it's easy but especially when it's hard. Keep growing. Keep loving. Keep showing up.

Because love that lasts isn't found. It's *built.*

And if you're both willing to build it brick by brick, day by day there's no storm you can't weather together.

Epilogue

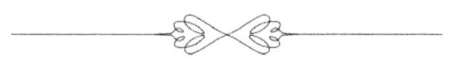

The Bridge Between Us

Understanding the way men communicate is not about changing who you are, nor is it about molding yourself into something unnatural. It is about bridging the gap about connection, respect, and appreciation for the way he expresses himself, even when his words seem few, and his actions speak volumes.

Throughout this journey, we've explored the nuances of the male code the unspoken rules, the instinctual responses, the silent struggles, and the profound ways men show love and commitment. We've examined how they handle emotions, conflict, and intimacy, and how they form bonds through shared experiences rather than verbal expression alone.

But the true power of this knowledge is not just in understanding men it's in fostering deeper, more meaningful relationships. When you listen beyond the words, when you appreciate the subtle gestures, when you create an environment where he feels safe to open up, you invite a kind of love that is built on trust, not just words.

No relationship is perfect, and no man no matter how emotionally intelligent will always communicate in a way that feels effortless. But with patience, awareness, and the willingness to see love through his lens, you gain access to a partnership that is stronger and more fulfilling.

As you move forward, remember that men may not always speak the way you expect, but they communicate in ways that matter. The key is not to change them, but to meet them where they are to honor both your differences and your similarities.

Love, after all, is not about deciphering a code. It is about choosing to understand, again and again.

www.ingramcontent.com/pod-product-compliance
Lightning Source LLC
Chambersburg PA
CBHW071515120626
46550CB00006B/2229

* 9 7 8 1 9 6 9 7 0 3 3 5 5 *